THE
INTERCESSION
OF
REES HOWELLS

THE INTERCESSION OF REES HOWELLS

**Readings from Rees Howells
with notes and introduction**

by

DORIS M. RUSCOE

 LUTTERWORTH PRESS
Guildford, Surrey, England

CHRISTIAN LITERATURE CRUSADE
Fort Washington, Pennsylvania 19034

LUTTERWORTH PRESS
Guildford, Surrey, England

First published in 1983
Copyright © Doris M. Ruscoe 1983

ISBN 0-7188-2585-3

CHRISTIAN LITERATURE CRUSADE
Fort Washington, Pennsylvania 19034

First published in 1983
Copyright © Doris M. Ruscoe 1983

ISBN-87508-467-2

Printed and bound in Great Britain by
Ebenezer Baylis & Son Limited
The Trinity Press, Worcester, and London

CONTENTS

Foreword

It was like climbing Mount Everest, the highest peak in my life, when God somehow led Rees Howells to invite me to visit him in his then newly-opened Bible College. We went for a walk together on the day of my arrival, and as he talked a great light lit within me. Here was a man by whom the Spirit was giving me illumination on a level I had never known before. It began a bond in the Spirit over the next twenty years. Looking back, I now know that this was God's means of giving me the Spirit-understanding by which alone I could and did fulfil his 'heavenly vision' to me in my Worldwide Evangelization Crusade calling. And it was during those years that the Lord also gave me the unique privilege of gathering together the main outlines of Rees Howells' life, helped by those who had lived with him in the college, and publishing in 1952 the book, *Rees Howells, Intercessor*, which still has such a wide circulation.

This has been translated into several languages, but in particular has been widespread in the USA. One outcome has been constant inquiries, by letters and when meeting people, 'Can you tell me more of what Rees Howells meant by Intercession?'

And now the answer has come through my contact with Miss Doris Ruscoe, who from its beginning in 1933 was headmistress of the school for missionaries' children, founded by Rees Howells. She is now retired but still lives at the school. I knew she had been deeply at one with Rees Howells throughout the years and I sensed that she, in association with Samuel Howells, son of Rees Howells and his successor in the directorship of the college, could give further insight in answer to this question.

For some time Miss Ruscoe had been considering the publication of extracts from the messages of Rees Howells, but I asked for fuller explanation and some account of life in the college with him, especially during the vital years of the Second World War, 1939–1945. This further development came as somewhat of a challenge but the Lord gave the word to go forward. Since doing so, in our various communications, Miss Ruscoe has again and again said that in this year of writing it has been as if she was lifted right out of herself in the Spirit, as she lived over again and recorded what had become so real to her through those years.

So here now is this Spirit-led record which has been given the title of *The Intercession of Rees Howells*.

I would say that this is no light book. Intercession is the highest calling the Spirit can fulfil by members of Christ's body, even as it was so perfectly fulfilled through the Great Intercessor (Hebrews 9.24). Likewise the apostle Paul pressed towards the fulfilment and reached it (Philippians 3.13, 14, and 2 Timothy 4.7). We tread on holy ground as we read these pages, but the same Spirit who is the Intercessor on earth today (Romans 8.26) does have his human intercessors, and any member of his redeemed body can have that highest calling, for all are of the 'royal priesthood' (1 Peter 2.9).

But surface concepts of Intercession – as, for instance, being just 'intercessory prayer' – are given their full dimension in that word of Rees Howells: 'He showed me he would put me on the Cross, but there would be a resurrection on the hundredfold.' As also he gave such a shock to the college community when, on a certain crisis occasion, he said, 'Prayer has failed and only Intercession will take us through.' Again when he spoke of Moses as 'prepared to sacrifice even his eternity to save his people,' and then, 'Others may give up, you cannot.'

Doris Ruscoe shows in detail how the Holy Spirit led Rees Howells, from his new birth onwards, to discover the principles of Intercession. She traces for us his earlier stages of learning and application, fascinating to those of us who by grace are being taken the same way. She leads on to the great intercession of World War Two, the intercession for the gospel to get to 'every creature', so marvellously being fulfilled before our eyes today, far beyond what he himself 'asked or thought' (Ephesians 3.20) when in the heat of the battle. In the end it was this intercession which did actually cost his physical body for he foresaw, a month before his day of glorification came, that God was taking him. Like the patriarch Jacob to his sons, he gave his word of commission to his son Samuel, and those who have continued with him, to persist in the fulfilment of this intercession; and Samuel Howells is right along with Miss Ruscoe in the writing and publishing of this book.

I am sure many will, as Paul said to the Ephesians, have 'the eyes of their understanding' newly enlightened as the Spirit speaks through these pages.

Norman P. Grubb

Acknowledgement

I would like to thank Miss Gladys Thomas, of The Evangelical School, Ramallah, who has read the manuscript from the beginning and sometimes given helpful advice on the arrangement of material. Also Miss Dorothy Davies of the Bible College of Wales, for her help with some of the typing.

Above all I am grateful for the constant support and encouragement of the Director of the Bible College, the Rev. Samuel R. Howells.

Doris M. Ruscoe

Preface

For a long time it has been our great desire that the teaching of Rees Howells, especially on the subject of Intercession, should be presented to the Christian world. The unique revelation of the indwelling person of the Holy Spirit, which he received in the mid-Wales Convention in 1906, was followed by a deep and costly path of preparation for what was ultimately to be a worldwide ministry. This was not to be in person, as he had sometimes thought might be the case, but rather through the biography *Rees Howells, Intercessor*, which has now been widely circulated throughout the world. As a result of this publication a growing interest in the ministry of Intercession has been aroused.

This book is the beginning of an effort to pass on to others the experience and teaching of Rees Howells on Intercession. Since the Lord took him in February 1950, the Bible College of Wales in Swansea, which he founded, has abundantly proved the power of Intercession in the world today. According to our Lord's words, 'the field is the world', and since 1950 the ministry of the college has been extended worldwide. Prayer and intercession for different lands are carried on unceasingly, and missionaries and national co-workers in many countries are being supported. Before his passing Rees Howells had the assurance that the intercession for finance had been gained, and hundreds of thousands of pounds have been sent out to the mission fields of the world during the past thirty years.

The fruits of Intercession are even now being seen in revival blessing in many regions. A great encouragement is the wonderful way that the Holy Spirit is working in the lands behind the Iron Curtain. This is an area on which the college has concentrated special intercession for many years.

We believe that this is a vital time for the power of Intercession to be brought to bear upon the many problems confronting the world today. We trust that this work will encourage Christians to unite in this ministry, and thereby prepare for the worldwide blessing and the outpouring of the Spirit on all flesh.

I trust that this book, which Miss Ruscoe has prepared, will be used to bring new light on some of the important principles of Intercession.

Samuel Rees Howells
Director, Bible College of Wales, Swansea

1

Reminiscences of Rees Howells
1933–1950

It was my privilege to be associated with Rees Howells in the years leading up to and during the Second World War of 1939–1945, the period in which he reached the peak of his ministry. Norman Grubb, author of *Rees Howells, Intercessor*, has asked me to give some account of life in the Bible College of Wales, Swansea, during those years, and I speak as a representative of the many staff and students who were in the college during the 1930s and 1940s.

I first came to the Bible College of Wales, Swansea, in 1932 as a visitor, together with my mother and my brother, Alfred Ruscoe, of the Worldwide Evangelization Crusade, whose life had been transformed through his contact with Rees Howells. After some years of local preaching in Derbyshire, and leading several Bible Study groups, I was spiritually 'dried up' and earnestly seeking to meet God in a new way. The Lord had revealed Calvary to me when I was a university student of nineteen and I had experienced the power of the Blood of Jesus, but in the Methodist circles in which I moved in the 1920s, the New Theology, especially the so-called 'higher criticism', had taken firm hold, and for several years the foundations of my faith were shaken. Was there in reality an absolute truth, on which one's life could be based with complete certainty and deep inner conviction? Apart from the Bible as the living Word of God there seemed to be only the shifting sands of varying interpretations and the theories of men with changing views. Was there this reality and if so where was it to be found? The answer came to me through Rees Howells in the Bible College of Wales, Swansea. It was

August. There was a heat wave, and the college was ostensibly on holiday, but in fact prayer and fasting were being carried on for several weeks, with prayer meeting after prayer meeting throughout the day and on into the evening. The meetings fascinated me. I was gripped with a sense of God's presence as never before, and the first time I heard Rees Howells speak I knew that here was a man who really knew God and knew him in a way I had never met in anyone else before. After a few days the opportunity came for a talk and prayer with the 'Director' as he was always called, and God met me in an overwhelming way. Shortly after he called me to the home and school for the children of missionaries, one of the special matters of prayer at that time. Within a year I resigned from the school in Matlock, Derbyshire, where I had been teaching for nine years, and moved with my mother to the college in Swansea. In September 1933 the school was started and it has been my home ever since.

Along with our ordinary work in college and school, we all, staff and students alike, sat at the feet of one whom God had led through strange and wonderful experiences, one who knew God in a direct and personal way and trusted him implicitly. While we were learning the rudiments of the life of faith, we saw Rees Howells reaching out to new heights, daily challenging us to trust God ourselves for the supply of personal needs, as his own faith rose to the needs of the college and school. We learned in the school of faith to pray with him prayers which became increasingly involved with a world vision and international affairs.

I can still see Rees Howells on that Boxing Day morning, December 26, 1934, as he came into the meeting in the old lecture hall, at 9 a.m. fresh from hours spent with the Lord, who had faced him with the challenge of believing that the Gospel could be given to 'every creature' in accordance with the last command of the Lord Jesus to 'go into all the world and preach the gospel to every creature' (Mark 16.28), and that this could be carried out in one generation. On New Year's Day, 1935, the college spent the whole day in prayer and fasting, as the reality and the implications of this command came home to all. From that day the 'Vision of Every

Creature' became the focal point of the life and prayers of the college. In the years that followed we were introduced in a practical way to the principles of Intercession. Henceforth we followed Rees Howells as the Holy Spirit began to prepare him for the warfare which lay ahead. There was a new concern for international affairs and as soon as Hitler came to power in Germany, it was revealed to Rees Howells that the devil, through this man, would seek world domination and so be a threat to the spread of the Gospel.

Those in the college at the time can never forget the burden in the spirit that came upon us when events in Europe were particularly threatening. Could anything stop the onward march of Hitler? He had established his supreme power in Germany and was already planning the achievement of his main objectives in Europe. As was usual, the college had been spending the weeks of Lent 1936 in prayer and fasting. Meetings took place throughout the day until late at night, with a break for a meal at 5 p.m. In the school we carried on with the normal routine but joined the college as far as possible in the midday meeting and in the evenings. Wearied we might be with the stresses and strains of the day in home and school, as well as very conscious of the burden that often weighed heavily upon us all, but over and over again in the meetings we were lifted into another realm and were renewed and refreshed day by day.

In March 1936 Hitler sent his troops into the Rhineland, an aggressive act which met with no resistance from any European power, nor from the League of Nations. But Rees Howells was profoundly disturbed in the spirit and a crisis came in the college on Sunday, March 29, a day never to be forgotten. Rees Howells came into the midday meeting not looking his usual self. Always immaculate, his hair was ruffled and on his face was a look of intense strain. He simply said, 'The Lord has told me that prayer has failed and only intercession will take us through.' We gazed at him, stunned and silent. Was it then really possible for prayer to fail – the intensive prayer of the recent weeks? What was the Lord asking of us? It was a new realm into which he was leading us and in the late meeting that night, we began to get light on the situation. The battle in the heavenlies was raging, the forces of darkness were gathering strength, the world was on the brink of disaster. What then of the Gospel to every creature? God had said through Isaiah that he wondered that there was no intercessor and in Ezekiel he had called for someone to stand in the gap. We began to see that the Holy Spirit was calling us to a total commitment to the heavenly warfare, to throw everything of ourselves into it.

Would we dare to enter this conflict and pledge ourselves not to let go until the tide of evil was thrown back and victory assured? Would we range ourselves on the side of the armies of heaven and follow whatever the cost? From 9 p.m. until midnight the Holy Spirit dealt with us as individuals, revealing to each one the price to be paid to take part in the intercession. We made our solemn vows to him and pledged ourselves not to withdraw until victory was won. We were aware that the Holy Spirit was leading through the Director and knew that he alone would know the cost to him to go through. For us all from that time on, spiritual matters, especially the battles of the Lord, the spiritual warfare, were always to take priority over everything else, whatever claims on time or strength there might be. Essentials must always be taken care of. In the school the standards of education and care for the children must never be lowered and they never were, but first and foremost we must follow the Holy Spirit as he led us in the Director.

In the years that followed the Holy Spirit held us to our vows. It involved weeks, even months, of prayer and fasting, with usually five meetings each day and no let-up at weekends or through the vacations. Hard on the flesh it was but who could estimate the spiritual gain? As a proof that the Holy Spirit had accepted the intercession of March 29, the days that followed were literally days of heaven upon earth. The Holy Spirit was poured out upon us and we prayed, sang and worshipped throughout the Easter vacation. From that time prayer was concentrated upon the international situation in a new way and continued through the years leading up to and during World War Two.

How the Holy Spirit led Rees Howells in those wonderful

years! Five meetings each day! How could anyone lead them and take them through? There were meetings when the Lord shed light on the great intercessors of the Bible, Moses, Daniel, Ezekiel, Nehemiah. There were quiet meetings when the Lord dealt deeply with us, revealing self, self-motive, things we had not realised were in us until the light of God showed them. Sometimes the Holy Spirit revealed himself in all his majesty and godhead, sometimes we were broken at the foot of the cross. At times the burden of prayer was heavy and it seemed impossible to break through the cloud of darkness and oppression, but we battled on and always at the end of the day there came a lifting in the Spirit and the assurance that in the end the victory would come. Before us always was the 'Vision of Every Creature', the preaching of the Gospel worldwide, the avoidance of war at all costs.

The meetings always began with Scripture and an address based on it, but obviously there could not be prepared messages. The only occasions when Rees Howells spoke in this way were the Sunday evenings when many people from the neighbourhood came for the Gospel Service at 6.30 p.m. He used to joke with us sometimes about his 'three heads' for his 'sermon' although he rarely kept close to them. But in the college meetings he always came with a definite leading from the Holy Spirit, a definite passage of Scripture, and often he used the well-known *Daily Light* readings. There was always a clear prayer objective and he relied upon the Holy Spirit to give light on the Word of God *as he spoke*. It was this which made the meetings often so exciting and so alive. From his early years when he had spent weeks and months alone with God and his Word, he had been given an insight into the lives of the men and women of the Bible, the way God had led them, their struggles of faith, their victories or failures and above all the paths of intercession along which they had been led.

Perhaps Rees Howells reached his greatest heights of Biblical exposition in dealing with the life of Moses. We were moved to our depths and taken into a realm hitherto unknown as the Holy Spirit, through Rees Howells, showed us a man on his face before God for 40 days and nights, prepared even to sacrifice his eternity for the sake of his people. It was God's dealings with these men, their positions of faith, their walk as intercessors, that enabled Rees Howells to attain to the faith he needed himself in his own dealings with God. Over and over again faith came in the actual meetings, while he was speaking, and as he 'went through' so did we along with him. In finance he had had to get the faith to buy property 'without money', something of which he had no experience before the purchase of Glynderwen, the first college property, and then Derwen Fawr, where the college was finally established. As he was led along the difficult path of liability to an ever deeper extent, and as he reached out in faith and intercession for the World Vision, every meeting was vital to him. Only as the Holy Spirit gave light on positions of faith as yet beyond him, which the men of the Bible had attained, was he able to accept the responsibility for the task given to him and to believe that God would take him through. We came to see what every meeting meant to him and that he needed our co-operation. It was necessary to concentrate on every word, to follow the line of thought and to trust the Holy Spirit to give us, up to our more limited capacity, the light he was giving him, and so be able to believe with him when the assurance came. Without that, the whole point of a meeting could be lost and it would be difficult to pick up the threads for the next meeting. This is why there was such a quality of life in the meetings as we, with him, reached out for the faith required for each crisis.

There were times when the Holy Spirit would break through with great light and give the assurance that the prayer was answered, or he would show us what God's purpose was. Then the hall was full of God's presence, and prayer turned to praise and worship. At times like these when there was such a release in the spirit, Rees Howells was never afraid to relax. For the time being, perhaps a day or two, he might cancel all the meetings and take two or three car-loads of us up to the Black Mountain and descend upon his cousins in a Welsh village for a real Welsh tea. When a break in the spirit came he would sometimes say that he 'shot out into space' and the glory of God was on him and we too tasted that joy of heaven which has to be experienced to be realised.

January 1937 brought never-to-be-forgotten days to the college when the person of the Holy Spirit was revealed, a revelation which came to staff and students alike, and which produced an indescribable awe in the presence of ineffable holiness and majesty. Day after day we were on our faces before him and often night was as day as his hand was upon us. Now we knew who was our real leader from this time forward, and we accepted his dealings, his discipline, his guidance, his commands, at whatever cost. There were times when he led us into deeper and deeper personal experiences of himself, into closer union and fellowship with the Lord Jesus, in his death and resurrection. To some the Easter of 1939 was specially memorable. The Director's messages were based on Romans 6, and for days the Holy Spirit rested on the college as one and another realised their identification with the Lord Jesus in his death and resurrection. As others joined our fellowship later, light was given on the words of the apostle Paul in Romans 12.1, 'I beseech you therefore brethren by the mercies of God, that ye present your bodies a living sacrifice, holy, acceptable unto God, which is your reasonable service.' The Holy Spirit made very real to every individual what it meant to be 'on that altar'. He was anointing us for the warfare in the heavenlies during the war years, and we were being drawn together into a closely-knit community, dedicated to fight the Lord's battles, concerned before everything else for the kingdom of God.

A feature of the college for many years was the annual *Every Creature Conference*, held in August, to which leaders of missions, missionaries and speakers from different parts of the world came. Many people had been blessed through the ministry of Rees Howells and the meetings were always crowded to overflowing throughout the week. There was always much blessing during the Conference and many responded to the call for full surrender to the Lord, or to the call for service. The conferences were discontinued during the war years and resumed afterwards. Rees Howells' last conference was in August 1949 and his messages were outstanding, with a conviction that the Holy Spirit would unite all believers in the great cause of world evangelisation.

2

The War Years, 1939–1945

Reference was made in the previous chapter to the way that from 1936 the college began to focus prayer on the international situation that was rapidly developing as Hitler tightened his grip on Germany, made an alliance with Mussolini in 1937 and in 1938 occupied Austria.

One of the most remarkable guidances of those pre-war years was the connection between the college and Ethiopia. Italy had long coveted Ethiopia and in October 1935 Mussolini ordered the invasion of the country. For various reasons no European country offered aid, and the League of Nations was too weak to intervene in an effectual way. Ethiopia fell to the Italians and the Emperor, Haile Selassie, became a fugitive in England. To Rees Howells this was a threat to the evangelisation of Ethiopia and much prayer was concentrated on the situation. Meanwhile Asrate Kassa, son of the great Ras Kassa, and a young man destined to play a great part in the government of his country, came as a boarder to the Bible College School, through Alfred Buxton of the Bible Churchman's Missionary Society. The Emperor visited the college and the school, and his private chaplain and his son-in-law, Abye Abebe, husband of the Princess Tshai who was doing nursing training in a London hospital, came as students to the Bible College.

Despite the apparent failure of the prayer for Ethiopia, Rees Howells assured the Emperor that the day would come when he would be restored to his country and to his throne. The Emperor came at times to the college meetings, a small but impressive figure with dark, penetrating eyes. In the summer of 1939 he and his party were camping with some of the students and schoolboys on the estate of Penllergaer, and when the European war broke out it was from there that he returned to London and then to his country and eventually to his throne. When he re-entered his capital city, Addis Ababa, he sent a cable to Rees Howells who replied, expressing his joy and promise of prayer for future peace. From that time they always exchanged greetings on the anniversary of the day when Haile Selassie re-entered Addis Ababa. One of the college doctors, Dr Margaret FitzHerbert was later decorated by the Emperor for her services to the women of Ethiopia. She became a consultant gynaecologist in the Princess Tshai Hospital in Addis Ababa and later worked in a leprosy hospital under the Sudan United Missionary society.

Some years later, in 1948, three cousins of the Kassa family, nephews of Asrate Kassa, now in high office in Ethiopia, came as boarders to the Bible College School. One of them, Hailou Desta Kassa, became an outstanding Christian leader in the school, and later a member of the Emperor's cabinet. A great Christian gentleman and statesman, he was looking forward to great things for his country, but he, along with two of his cousins, also Asrate Kassa and Abye Abebe, were all murdered by the revolutionary government in 1975 when every member of the Emperor's government was executed in one night.

Also in the pre-war years occurred a development which was to occupy a large share of the college prayers, and to lead to another great intercession. In 1938, Hitler began to persecute the Jews on an unprecedented scale and there were many Jewish orphans whose parents had been taken away to a then unknown fate. The love of the Holy Spirit in him for the orphans of the Welsh village, was now manifested through Rees Howells for these children. Efforts were made to rescue some from the Continent. Some were adopted into the college family, others came into the home and school for the children of missionaries. Early in January 1939 Rees Howells called a special day of prayer for the Jewish people and this was to prove the beginning of the intercession which was to continue right through the war and beyond, until the

23

day when Israel became a nation in 1948.

New light was given on the prophecies of Isaiah, Jeremiah, Ezekiel and others, as frequently in the meetings he read the great prophecies of the future restoration and greatness of Israel, and prayer was never relaxed for their fulfilment.

The first great war crisis occurred in September 1939, through the Nazi threat to Czechoslovakia. To Rees Howells war was the major threat to the vision of reaching every creature with the Gospel in this generation. Historians have continued to debate the wisdom, even the morality, of the Munich Agreement, when the British Prime Minister, Neville Chamberlain, returned to London from his interview with Hitler, with his 'scrap of paper' and his declaration of 'peace in our time'. We prayed right through this crisis, and before the Prime Minister returned we had the assurance that war had been averted for the time being.

Never was the Holy Spirit more manifest in the college than in the month of August 1939. Over and over again we were taken 'beyond the veil' in the meetings, and over and over again we were lost in a spirit of praise, and worship. Rees Howells was confident that there would be no war and believed this right up to the fatal day of September 3 when war was declared because of the Nazi attack on Poland. He was always like a lion in a test, but as he went back to the Lord day after day seeking an explanation, the conviction grew within him that God had a purpose in the war, that without it the three great dictators, Hitler, Mussolini and Stalin would override the world. During the next months of what came to be known as 'the phoney war' because there was little action of vital importance on either side, he produced a small book, *God Challenges the Dictators*. From the beginning he pronounced 'the doom of the dictators', committing himself to this in an absolute and final way. However dark the situation might be he never swerved from this commitment and held on to it throughout the years of war. Assured that the war could not last long he predicted its end by the following Whitsuntide, May 1940, the very time when Hitler's Panzer regiments broke through the Allied lines and began to roll over Europe. The European war had begun in earnest. On Whit Monday crowds flocked to the college meetings held in the open air, many curious, most disbelieving. Was it failure? To the press, to the crowds, there could be no other conclusion, but as Rees Howells went back to the Lord, he began to understand. The great principle of Intercession is life out of death; the corn of wheat must die before the new life can spring forth from the ground. Rees Howells saw the glory that would have come to himself and the college if the prediction had come to pass. He said, 'The glory and the credit for victory in this war must come to the Holy Spirit and not to man. God has declared war on the devil and it is God who will give the victory.'

Hitler boasted that he would set up a Nazi regime throughout the world which would last for a thousand years, a direct challenge to the Millennial Reign of Christ. Rees Howells took this public 'death' with perfect acceptance as from God and threw himself into the battle against the dictators, the conflict in the heavenlies, and we followed him with complete confidence in the final victory. There were to be days of darkness, oppression and burden in the spirit, but also days when we were caught up into those heavenly places of which the apostle Paul speaks, days of heaven upon earth. From the human standpoint it is clear that an early and abrupt end to the war would have left the dictators, their governments and their armies still strong and powerful, still a threat to the world. To us it seemed that we were baptised into the conflict in a new way. Rees Howells never defended the prediction of 1940. He was not new to this kind of 'death' and knew that in the end there would be a resurrection. He reiterated 'the doom of the Nazis' and of the dictators and carried on the struggle of faith with ever deeper conviction. The crowds were no longer interested in the college and for the next few years we were literally shut in with God.

Day by day Rees Howells wrestled with the Word of God, especially the positions of faith of the men of the Old Testament, believing that God is the same today and that the Holy Spirit could be equal to these positions today. We saw the setbacks that Moses experienced in Egypt as the enemy through Pharaoh and the magicians defied him. But Moses knew that

God had one final weapon that would bring about the deliverance of the people from Egypt – deliverance through the death of the firstborn. In the days of Hezekiah God allowed the enemy to take all the fenced cities of Judah and to come right up to the walls of Jerusalem itself before he spoke the word of deliverance through the prophet Isaiah, that God himself would defend the city for his own sake. The strange plot of Judges 20 demonstrated the mystery of God's ways in some situations. Twice the men of Judah asked counsel of God and went up against Benjamin, only to be driven back each time with great slaughter. But after a national day of prayer and fasting the word of assurance was given and victory came on the third attempt. So throughout those years, in a real war situation, the Word of God came alive to us in a new way and daily the Holy Spirit sustained us as we fought on, knowing that the real battle was in the heavenlies, and over and over again seeing the outcome of a spiritual victory demonstrated later in the actual fighting.

For some time the evening meeting had been extended from 6 p.m. until 9 p.m. but when the war began in earnest there were two meetings every night, from 7 p.m. until 9 p.m. and from 10 p.m. until midnight and usually long after. Most of the meetings were in the Conference Hall but the last meeting was always in what was known as the Blue Room. How sacred this room was to become to us as night after night the Holy Spirit gave light on the Word and lifted us up above the burdens of the day. As Rees Howells said, why should we be freer in our part of the conflict than those who were engaged in the fighting on land, sea and in the air? Because of conscription for military service, it became no longer possible for the college to function in the normal way, and lectures were suspended until after the war. Over and over again the Holy Spirit broke through in the meetings with new revelations of divine grace and renewed assurance of final victory. At such times we sang and sang, hymns of praise and worship, sometimes even national songs, especially in the late meeting in the Blue Room. There were soldiers in a camp in a field nearby and we used to wonder sometimes what they thought of us when they heard the singing.

As each crisis in the war developed, the Holy Spirit guided our prayers and each time we knew that victory had been gained in the spirit before news came over the radio or in the newspapers of victory on the field of battle. Apart from the Holy Spirit, how did we know each time beforehand when and where victory would come, or where particularly to direct prayer upon specific situations? The year 1940 saw a desperate situation. As European country after country fell to the enemy so the spiritual darkness seemed to go deeper and deeper. So great was the burden that there were times when Rees Howells could only wrestle alone with God in his room, while members of the staff carried on with the meetings. Some of the events of those years are written on our hearts. Who among us could forget the prayers for the British army cut off at Dunkirk and whose escape seemed impossible? The prayer of Tommy Howells in one meeting was like the agonised prayer of Mordecai in the time of Queen Esther. That cry surely reached the throne. A solemn group of us gathered round the radio one night and heard of the fall of France, the treachery of Mussolini and the courageous challenge made by our own King George VI. How we praised God for a king and queen who were dedicated Christians and who could lead the nation in prayer. Several times national days of prayer were called for in those critical years when civilisation itself seemed to be threatened, and Britain stood alone.

There were also times of tremendous victory. During the Battle of Britain, in the autumn of 1940, when Britain stood alone against the enemy and our airmen were fighting desperately to withstand the enemy attacks, especially on London, Rees Howells said, 'Christian England will never be invaded.' The enemy offensive, intended as a preliminary to invasion, came to a climax on September 15, a day we remember again for the assurance of victory. The attack failed and the invasion did not take place.

One of the outstanding guidances of the war occurred in 1941. There was a night when Rees Howells announced that the Lord had told him that Hitler's forces were to be turned south towards the Mediterranean area and also that he was preparing to attack Russia. No such eventuality was indicated in any way at the time, but several weeks later, the telephone rang in the school on a Sunday morning, and I heard the voice of Rees Howells from the college. 'Have you heard the news this morning? Hitler has attacked Russia.' The war on the Russian Front was watched closely and prayer concentrated as the Lord directed. I still have a newspaper cutting of December 22, 1941. 'Moscow was ready to fight to the last. Mystery of Nazi failure. It is still too early to say how Moscow was saved from capture in the middle of October and again in the encircling movement that followed. It was a miracle.' A miracle indeed, but after intensive prayer the Lord had given us beforehand the assurance that Moscow would not fall. It seemed that the Holy Spirit was always ahead of the enemy. Outstanding again was the victory at Stalingrad, a city that the enemy had actually entered, and fierce fighting was going on in the streets. As we prayed it seemed that the Holy Spirit took us right into the city and drove the enemy out himself. It was the first time they had lost a city into which their troops had actually entered.

Why should there be so much prayer for the city of Stalingrad? The war had spread to North Africa and the Holy Spirit made it clear to Rees Howells that Palestine itself, the Holy Land, was in danger, threatened by a pincer movement from two directions. If Rommel took Cairo and then the German forces swept south through Russia, the fate of the Holy Land would be sealed and there would be no prospect of a national home for the Jewish people when the war was over. So the enemy was held back in Russia. When the war came to a head in North Africa, and the vital battle of El Alamein was taking place, we were on our knees all day and it was in the afternoon meeting that the Lord assured us of victory, a victory confirmed later as we heard of the success of the Allied forces under Montgomery.

One aspect of the war concerned us in a more personal way. Swansea, in South Wales, is a big industrial centre, with factories then supplying important war materials, and it has a large oil refinery on its outskirts. It is also a port with large docks, and when the seas of Eastern Europe were closed to

British shipping, because the enemy controlled the seaways of Norway, Denmark, Holland, Belgium and France, from 1940 onwards, the Western Approaches were of vital importance for essential supplies of food and materials. After the fall of France in June 1940, Britain stood alone until the entry of the United States of America into the war at the end of 1941. For months all our industrial cities and ports were heavily bombed and Swansea did not escape. When the air raids began, Rees Howells was in a dilemma. All the property was the Lord's and each building was a monument to his faithfulness in answer to prayer. Could we ask him then to protect us as he had his people in times past? Should we use air raid shelters? Rees Howells would never take unnecessary risks and always sought a word from the Lord in uncertainty. We can never forget the evening meeting when the Lord spoke clearly through Exodus 12.13, 'and when I see the blood I will pass over you.' From that night we had the absolute assurance that no harm would come to any of the buildings and that we ourselves were safe under that precious blood, so much more precious than the blood of the Passover sacrifice.

It was an eerie feeling sometimes to hear the whirr of enemy planes directly above us and the sound of exploding bombs. Sometimes we would look out of upstairs windows and see in the distance the fires lighting up the dock area, a constant centre of attack, or watch the fires in buildings nearer at hand in the city. But from that night none of us went into shelters except for the children in the day school, in accordance with government regulations, which insisted upon adequate shelters for certain buildings, especially schools. Civilians were not allowed out on the streets during an air raid apart from the wardens whose duty it was to watch the streets and look for casualties. The school had many day pupils as well as the missionary boarders, and although the heaviest raids were usually at night, they did occur in daylight hours, especially in the earlier days of the war. It became commonplace for lessons to be disrupted and sometimes they had to be continued in the shelters provided.

Most of our missionary boarders had to remain with us throughout the war. They could not return to their parents during the school vacation, nor could their parents visit them. Travel was unsafe even in this country and submarine warfare made sea voyages dangerous. But the Lord provided wonderfully for those children, not least during the times of strict food rationing. On special occasions particularly at Christmas delicacies which most people did not see until after the war, appeared from nowhere.

At night during the raids some of our older boarders held prayer meetings in their dormitories for their friends in the city. One of the day girls used to read Psalm 91 to her family as they spent the night in their shelter. Many of our day pupils, as well as the boarders, had been greatly blessed in the later weeks of 1940, as the Holy Spirit brought revival blessing to the school. It was a wonderful preparation for the testing times that followed, when the heavy raids occurred.

One night will always remain in my memory. When the sirens sounded the warning of the approach of enemy planes, it was my custom to fall on my knees and pray for the children. Their missionary parents were far away, unable to return home. In one bedroom were several small girls, aged between five and eight years, and that night, as I prayed, the Holy Spirit showed me that room full of the presence of God and I saw those little ones literally sleeping in God. From that night the school building, Glynderwen, was always to me the safest place in Swansea. Some of these young children slept through even the heaviest raids, although there was a very noisy anti-aircraft gun-emplacement a few yards down the road. One morning, a little girl said to the School Matron, 'It was very windy last night, wasn't it, matron?' Actually Swansea experienced one of the exceptionally heavy raids, three attacks, directed against all the major ports, and it was an awesome sight to watch the flares lighting up the sky, to see the fires from the heavy bombs and the rain of incendiaries upon the city, making one think of Sodom and Gomorrah. The centre of the city was completely wrecked and had to be rebuilt in later years. There was also heavy loss of life. Yet not a bomb was dropped on college or school property although they fell on the area immediately surrounding us. The container of a burnt-out flare was the only relic of many a raid.

So prayer continued throughout the war years. Early in 1944 it was known generally that the Second Front was being prepared by the Allies and that an invasion of France was imminent. Rees Howells was troubled. He took nothing for granted in a crisis and in his mind were the difficulties at Dunkirk in 1940 and the more recent commando raid at Dieppe which had failed, with great loss of life. He went back to the Lord and the word came, 'This will not be like Dunkirk, Tobruk or Singapore. I am going before the forces.' Could we believe that the Lord would give victory where formerly there had been defeat? Once again the Holy Spirit gave the assurance of victory and on the night of the Allied invasion, the thousands of ships and troops got across the Channel almost unobserved. Rees Howells always looked back on this night as another instance of divine aid. Truly, God had gone on before and there could be no failure. One newspaper reported that it was the only night that enemy submarines did not patrol the Channel. There were desperate days while the Second Front was being established in Normandy, and hard fighting in the ensuing weeks and months, but the Lord had said there would be no setbacks this time and we followed the conflict in prayer day by day until the final victory.

Rees Howells had maintained throughout that there would be a divine intervention in this war because God himself was engaged in it. Whatever form this might take, God's ways are not always our ways not are his thoughts always our thoughts as Isaiah says. Rees Howells said, 'It has been a divine intervention all along but people have not seen it.' Kings, great leaders, statesmen and generals, united with people throughout the world to give thanks to God for the deliverance. We can always say, as we look back on those years, that we saw the hand of God at work in crisis after crisis, that he guided and directed our prayers and gave us the assurance of victory. Hitler and Mussolini did not survive the war and although Stalin continued in power for a few years his death in 1953 was followed by Kruschev's denunciation of the Stalin cult.

There is no doubt that these were the years when the ministry of Rees Howells reached its greatest heights, but his health had been seriously impaired by the strain and burden of the war. Over and over again the Spirit revived him and gave him the strength so that in every crisis he was 'on the bridge' directing the battle and never letting go until the final victory.

After the war, when the college re-opened to students and normal life continued, the Holy Spirit laid on Rees Howells a special burden for the Jewish people and especially for their establishment in Palestine. After the holocaust of the Nazi years and the movement of the Jews back to 'the Land', the Lord still further opened up to Rees Howells the prophecies concerning his chosen people. The troubles under the British mandate were followed with great concern, but as it drew to a close the Jewish question became an issue in the United Nations. We prayed fervently that God's people might at last be granted a home of their own in the land which God had promised to Abraham, to Isaac and to Jacob. In a wonderful meeting in the Blue Room one night in 1947, when the crucial vote for the partitioning of Palestine was to be cast in the United Nations, the Holy Spirit came upon Rees Howells and us all. We saw the angels of God surrounding the UNO building in San Francisco and had the assurance that God would overrule any attempt to thwart his plan for his own people. Great was the rejoicing when the vote went in favour of giving at least part of the land to the Jewish people and there was special rejoicing later when we heard that Israel was to be a nation again after 2000 years, and in its own land.

In the remaining months of his life two prayers particularly claimed the attention of Rees Howells: the prayer for China, about to be taken over by the Communist forces under Mao Tse Tung, and above all, the intercession for the financing of the vision of the Gospel to every creature. Throughout the war years the Lord wonderfully sustained the college financially and sent in many thousands of pounds, although little if any time was given to praying for finance in the college meetings. In a literal way we proved that if we 'seek first the Kingdom of God and his righteousness, all these things shall be added.' On Sunday, January 15, 1950, just four weeks before his home call, the final assurance of victory in the intercession for finance came. He believed that his prayer for £100,000 would be granted and that no lack of finance would hinder the outreach of the Gospel in the world.

His death was a traumatic experience for the college but we all rallied round his son, Rev. Samuel Rees Howells, on whom the Spirit came to continue the work of the college and to fulfil the intercession.

3

Introduction to the Readings

Rees Howells was above all a man of faith and of the Holy Spirit. To him the Bible was the Word of God and daily he drew fresh inspiration from its pages. He always needed a new copy of the Bible every year, usually at Christmas time, and by the following November its pages were becoming loosened and worn with constant use. He never theorised on the Word. To him it was a practical guidebook and as the writer to the Epistle to the Hebrews says, 'quick and powerful and sharper than any two edged sword, piercing even to the dividing asunder of soul and spirit, and of the joints and marrow, and is a discerner of the thoughts and intents of the heart' (Hebrews 4.12). He taught us to read it daily on our knees and to look to the Holy Spirit to give us light and understanding and guidance from its pages. As it was life to him so it became life to us.

From the day that the Holy Spirit met him in the Convention in mid-Wales at Llandrindod Wells (often called the Welsh Keswick), in 1906, Rees Howells was always reaching out in faith to embrace the will of God, first in his own personal life and then for its fulfilment for God's people throughout the world. The meetings in the college became an essential part of this and he came to them expecting to gain more light on the Word from the Holy Spirit and more faith for the prayer on hand. To him *prayer* meant *answer*, and no prayer was ever to be undertaken lightly because he felt responsible for the answer. This largely accounts for the continual challenge in the meetings, a challenge to go further with God, to believe more strongly.

Sometimes, especially in the Blue Room meetings, he would directly challenge individuals, particularly his faithful friend of many years, Thomas Howells (known to the children in the school as Uncle Tommy), 'Well, Tommy, are you believing?' He had a great sense of humour and often delighted us with his stories. We all felt the love of God expressed through him and we loved and honoured him as our father in God. Always in complete control of the meetings, he was highly sensitive to the Spirit and brooked no disturbance or lack of concentration. Each meeting was meaningful to him as he grappled in faith with some world issue.

The experience of the New Birth and the revelation of the person of the Holy Spirit were the foundation of his spiritual life. Over the years he was deeply taught by the Spirit, who led him into that realm of Intercession with which he became identified. He made this life so attractive that all we desired was to enter into it ourselves, to experience something of the same depths of fellowship with God that he experienced, at whatever cost. This he never minimised, and there were times when he led us into that Holy of Holies where we stood in awe at the revelation of the depths of our Lord's atoning sacrifice, or were overwhelmed by an experience of the glory of God.

For a number of years detailed notes of the college meetings were taken by the secretaries, especially Miss Mary Henderson, the personal secretary of Rees Howells. These readings are taken mainly from her notes and from others taken at the time.

Rees Howells and the New Birth

Except a man be born again, he cannot see the kingdom of God.   John 3.3

Some of the Saviour's most vital truths were spoken to individuals, such as Nicodemus and the woman at the well. Nicodemus represented the Jews of his day and his concern was to know why the Saviour had the power to do what no one else could do. The first thing the Lord said to him upset him. 'Except a man be born again he cannot see the kingdom of God.' You may believe many things about the Bible, but this is still true that you cannot see the kingdom of God unless you are born again. Measure yourself with this man, this ruler of the Jews. Keeping the law does not get you into the kingdom. There was probably a greater conflict in this than you ever thought. The Saviour came to open a new dispensation and what changes there would have to be from former times. He was doing a new thing altogether and doing away with the sacrifices on which their worship had been based for so many generations. Nicodemus represented the synagogue, and in this conversation the Saviour gave to him the main principle of his teaching: 'as Moses lifted up the serpent in the wilderness even so must the Son of man be lifted up' (John 3.14). It was not *religion* that Nicodemus needed but *life*.

As many as received him, to them gave he power to become the sons of God.   John 1.12

Under the old dispensation no one called God 'Father.' How can you do this until you are born of God? People pray, 'Our Father' when they are not born of him and they say, 'Give us this day our daily bread,' and they do not trust him. Although I used the name 'Father' before I was born of him there was no real meaning in it to me. It was not so much a new teaching that the Saviour brought but a new relationship. Teaching will not make you any different from Judaism. Only through birth can you take the likeness of the one you are born of.
Before I was born again I thought that only men who indulged in the world were sinners. I had been brought up in a most religious home and always believed the

Bible. I lived a most religious life, a better life by nature than many by grace. The Incarnation, the atonement, the resurrection: I believed all these but I was still carrying my sins. When someone asked me, 'Have you been born again?', I said, 'What do you mean?' I was only 23 when I became very ill in America and for the first time faced death. How dark it was. I found that all I had was an historical Christ and not a personal Saviour. For five months I lived in the fear of death. I was facing an Eternity and I did not know what was beyond death. Then I met the Saviour and I saw that he came into the world to die on Calvary for me, that he fulfilled the Law and I was free. I never once had fear of death after that. Oh, the liberty I came into! I was never to be condemned. God has given me great gifts but none to be compared with the gift of Eternal Life.

He that hath the Son hath life and he that hath not the Son of God hath not life.   1 John 5.12

There is nothing greater than to be born of God, born into the kingdom. Is there anything greater than to be a child of the Highest? I believe that many have only given a mental assent to these things. I had believed in him before, but when I saw him I broke down at the foot of the Cross and I never recovered. I have always said that the moment you have seen Calvary you can do nothing else but give your life to him. The new birth is greater than you ever dreamed of. Although you are in the world you are not of the world.

When a person who has not seen the Cross talks about it, it is only words. I knew the moment when I saw Calvary, and nothing has remained with me as that has. I saw that the Saviour was God and that he came to

37

make an atonement for me. He said, 'I gave my life for you. What are you going to give back to me?' I said, 'My life,' and he said, 'Will you let me in?' I opened the door and he came in and I entered into another world altogether. I knew that I was born of God in a moment of time and I did not want one thing that the world could offer. God became my Father, and how sweet that was. It was as natural now for me to call God 'Father', as it was beforehand to call my natural father 'father'. Could you put a doubt in me that I had not changed from this world into the other world? From this time I was at home in the presence of God with Life Eternal.

The hour is coming in the which all that are in the graves shall hear his voice, and shall come forth; they that have done good, unto the resurrection of life; and they that have done evil, unto the resurrection of damnation. John 5.28,29

Even before I met the Saviour a stillness used to come over me on Easter Sunday. I used to think of that first Easter morning when the Saviour rose from the dead and to realise that one day all that are in the graves will hear his voice and be called out, either to Life Eternal or to damnation. These are truths whether you like them or not. You must face Eternity sooner or later. When I faced death I realised that I had not prepared for Eternity and I cried to God to deliver me from death and to give me one more chance. Suppose you knew that you were to face death tomorrow. Would you be ready for it? There is only one thing that can make a man go to a lost eternity and that is, rejecting the Saviour; only one sin that can take a person down to hell and that is, refusing the atonement. He came for all the world, to give Life to every person. He said, 'I am come that they might have life, and that they might have it more abundantly' (John 10.10). He offers his risen Life to all who would believe. When I saw that he, who was perfect God and perfect man, left glory to die on the Cross for me, my whole being went out to him. I loved and worshipped him, I accepted him and I became a son of God, adopted into the family of God.

But seek ye first the kingdom of God, and his righteousness.   Matthew 6.33

If the least in the kingdom is greater than John the Baptist (Luke 7.28), then there is a standard of life in this, the standard of the Sermon on the Mount. I went to America to make money but I lost all that when I was born again. The new life is stronger than the old life and you grow in it. I never tried to live for the Saviour or to grow spiritually, but as in nature the new life pushes out the old, so I lost the things of the world. You come to live in a world where your soul is fed and there is a sweetness, a peace, that the world can never give. Have you this real foundation, this real fellowship? When the Lord Jesus, the Risen Lord, came into my life my one passion was to tell others of the gift I had received; my one ambition was to do back for him what he had done for me. He was the Good Shepherd and laid down his life for the sheep, and as the apostle John says, 'we ought to lay down our lives for the brethren' (1 John 3.16). It is only in so far as the death of the Saviour is real to you that it will have an effect upon others through you.

God is a Spirit and they that worship him must worship him in spirit and in truth.   John 4.24

Before you can worship in spirit and in truth the God who is a spirit, you must be born of the Spirit. These things have been taken as teaching but they are not real to you unless they have been revealed to you. Nothing about God is real to you unless it has been revealed. Otherwise it is speculation. John the Baptist said, 'I saw, and bare record that this is the Son of God' (John 1.34). The proof of this was that his ministry finished when the Saviour came. He could never have given a better picture than that of the bridegroom and the friend. The bridegroom had come and the friend's ministry had finished. The Saviour revealed himself to Nicodemus and to the woman at the well and it must be a revelation today. The woman believed that Jesus would give her water different from that in the well. Reason and intelligence alone cannot take these spiritual things in.

Rees Howells and the Holy Spirit

I beseech you therefore, brethren, by the mercies of God, that ye present your bodies a living sacrifice, holy, acceptable unto God, which is your reasonable service.   Romans 12.1

No single person can receive the Holy Spirit until he has made a full and complete surrender. He is a person, and when he comes in, he brings in all that is of God, and from that time it is in God you live and not to any selfish motives. I never once sought a blessing after he came in; I had the blesser himself. It may take you some time to get used to this new realm but do not try to do anything of yourself. When he wants to do something through you, he will make it plain. You need to realise your position in him: 'Blessed be the God and Father of our Lord Jesus Christ, who hath blessed us with all spiritual blessings in heavenly places in Christ' (Ephesians 1.3). Live with him, come to know him and allow him to speak to you. When you have the Holy Spirit, you do not need to make a show. He will reveal himself without your effort. It is a new realm altogether, a realm in which you are 'transformed by the renewing of your mind, that ye may prove what is that good and acceptable, and perfect, will of God' (Romans 12.2). This life in the Holy Spirit is as simple as it is great.

The Spirit of truth; whom the world cannot receive, because it seeth him not, neither knoweth him: but ye know him; for he dwelleth with you, and shall be in you.   John 14.17

The Holy Spirit is not an influence but a divine person, the third person of the Godhead, with all the attributes of a person: will, intelligence, power and love. He is the only witness on earth today of the Saviour and of Calvary, and he is the only one who can made God's will known to you.

We do not know these things until they are revealed to us and at the 1906 Llandrindod Wells Convention in Wales, he was revealed to me, and I saw him. I had lived for the Saviour for three and a half years and longed to give my life back to him. The first morning of the convention, the Holy Spirit spoke to me. 'You hath he quickened and hath raised you up to sit with Christ

41

in heavenly places.' It was the crucified Christ I had seen before but now I had a vision of the glorified Christ and only one glimpse of that is enough for eternity. I saw myself sitting with the one I loved throughout eternity, and like the apostle Paul I was dazzled, and all the things of the earth grew strangely dim. 'Eye hath not seen, nor ear heard, neither have entered into the heart of man, the things which God hath prepared for them that love him. But God hath revealed them unto us by his Spirit' (1 Corinthians 2.9, 10). I believe my experience was like that of the prophet Isaiah. He saw God and saw himself. He said, 'Woe is me! for I am undone; because I am a man of unclean lips and I dwell in the midst of a people of unclean lips' (Isaiah 6.5). The Holy Spirit then appeared to me and said, 'I am the one who revealed that position to you and I want a body to dwell in to reveal the Saviour through you.' I saw that he was God, that he was holy, pure, divine, and I was a man with a sinful nature. Before that experience I had never seen myself. All that I had by nature was self, a self I had cultivated and kept under, a self the Holy Spirit would not live with.

He showed me what it would mean if he came in. The verse he gave me was, 'Know ye not that so many of us as were baptised into Jesus Christ were baptised into his death?' (Romans 6.3). As really as the Saviour died on that Cross, I would have to die before my nature was changed. Whether it is 'good self' or 'bad self' it is still self and must go to the Cross. I had received a sentence of death as really as a prisoner in the dock. For seven days he dealt with me. My will would have to go; I would never have another choice, and I was never to question him in thought, word or motive. Each day he cleansed and purged me so that I could never go back again to my former life, and finally he gave me one hour to decide whether I, myself, was to live on, or he was to live in me. My destiny for eternity depended on that hour. At last I said, 'Lord, I am willing,' and he came in. He did not force the decision on me: I had to decide. I was carried right into the presence of God and the verse he gave me was: 'Having therefore, brethren, boldness to enter into the holiest by the blood of Jesus' (Hebrews 10.19). From that time on there was a line drawn between my old life and this new one. Like John the Baptist, I had to decrease and he had to increase.

The Holy Ghost, whom God has given to them that obey him.   Acts 5.32

It is exactly the same for a man who is born again to receive the Holy Spirit as for a man who is not born again to receive the Saviour. He is given to them that obey. It is his all for your all. Suppose you have a property of a hundred acres and you wish to sell all except the one acre right in the middle. The new owner might resent your walking over his property and might even take you to law about it, but the verdict would be, 'If he has one acre in the middle he must have a right of way to it.' If you withhold just one acre of your life from the Holy Spirit, the devil will find not one way of getting to it, but many. The Holy Spirit comes in to take full possession. Your life is like a plot of land, marred and made barren by the Fall, and cannot bring forth fruit unto God. The Holy Spirit will begin to work on it, one acre at a time, until he has dealt with it all. You cannot play with him. Those who have no fear of the Holy Spirit have never seen him. I had far more fear of him than I had of my old schoolmaster when I was a boy in school. He will never take second place to self or the devil, and he will not dispute with you. I never once minimised the third person of the Godhead. When he comes in, God comes in and he will not mix with your sinful nature. You are to die *to* sin as really as the Saviour died *for* sin.

He that loveth his life shall lose it and he that hateth his life in this world shall keep it unto life eternal. John 12.25

When you have given up your life entirely to the Holy Spirit you have no right to take it back or to resent what he does with it. You will have no more claim on your life yourself, and you accept everything from him, whether it seems to be for you or against you. The surrender of outward things is only the beginning. When he comes in, he shows you yourself as he sees you and he deals with the old nature, its thoughts and motives. Human reasoning and understanding belong to the old nature which God tells us not to trust (Proverbs 3.5). You must learn to be quiet before God for him to show you these things. At one time I spent three hours with him and the Word every evening for several months and he dealt with every thought and motive of self.

And behold I send the promise of my Father upon you: but tarry ye in the city of Jerusalem until ye be endued with power from on high . . . and they worshipped him, and returned to Jerusalem with great joy: and were continually in the temple praising and blessing God. Luke 24.49, 52, 53

Joy is not the proof that the Holy Spirit has come, nor

are sorrow and testing proofs that he has not come. The disciples were rejoicing in the knowledge of eternal life and the forgiveness of sins, but they needed power for service. It is as unreasonable for a missionary to go out without the power of the Holy Spirit as it is for a minister who is not born again to preach the Gospel. The Spirit will change your nature and change your motives so that you may live entirely for him.

He may not give you anything to do for some time but you will have the realisation daily that he is in you, and you will have more fellowship with him than with anyone else. Just live with him and come to know him. When you are 'in God' your position with him is a million times greater than anything he does through you. We are so apt to be active but when he wants to do something through you, he will do it. The realisation that he was in me was so great that it affected everyone I met. There was great joy when my eldest brother was converted, and many of us who were born again had great fellowship together, but when the Holy Spirit came into my life it was different. Some of my friends did not want him and he had no fellowship with them. Once the Holy Spirit has taken you into the presence of God you have more fellowship on 'the other side' than down here. Put the man of God where you like but if God is there it is heaven upon earth.

Knowing this, that our old man is crucified with him, that the body of sin might be destroyed, that henceforth we should not serve sin.   Romans 6.6

Self cannot put self on the Cross: only the Holy Spirit can do this. If the death of the Lord Jesus is real to you, will you go to Calvary with him? It is not weeping for the death 2000 years ago but being willing to go to death yourself. I have never tried to show Calvary in words. It must be a revelation. Death must work in you and then life, and just to the extent you allow him to put you to death you will live. With many, the planting into the death of the Saviour is only a theory. You only understand his death as you enter into it in reality. The apostle Paul said, 'I am crucified with Christ: nevertheless I live; yet not I, but Christ liveth in me' (Galatians 2.20). Anyone who has really seen Calvary is lost to the world. You must get rid of sin and limitations: the death must be actual. The law will not be satisfied with theory. It is when you die to the law of sin and death that you are free (Romans 8.2). After you are baptised by the Holy Spirit into the death of the Saviour you then walk in newness of life.

Some people live in the forgiveness of sins. Just as interest can be paid out of capital, some people do this spiritually. If you reckon yourself dead to sin you have no right to live in it. The only proof of the Holy Spirit is the life of the Holy Spirit. Leave 'the old man' on the Cross and rise with the Saviour to a new life.

For if we have been planted together in the likeness of his death, we shall be also in the likeness of his resurrection.   Romans 6.5

This life is not a death life but a resurrection life. Jesus said, 'I am the resurrection and the life', and if you are in him you are in the resurrection. The prayer of the apostle Paul was, 'That I may know him, and the power of his resurrection, and the fellowship of his sufferings, being made conformable unto his death' (Philippians 3.10). Suffering is the very thing the 'old man' will run away from. 'For if we be dead with him we shall also live with him: if we suffer we shall also reign with him' (2 Timothy 2.11, 12). The way to the throne is always the way of the Cross. The devil only has power on this side of Calvary. The Saviour always had power over him, but he came to conquer him, so that the Saviour through man might ever have the victory over him. The Holy Spirit comes in with all the power of the risen Lord and he in me constantly had victory over the enemy. The Holy Spirit was constantly binding the devil.

***

Now thanks be unto God, which always causeth us to triumph in Christ, and maketh manifest the saviour of his knowledge by us in every place.   2 Corinthians 2.14

You must see that you get victory in every change that the Holy Spirit makes in you. I had victory in every situation. You will not be tested in the open unless you have had victory on that point in private. God can always test his own faith but not the faith of man. You cannot hold out in a test without a revelation. Whatever you give to God, if you believe for it, you will have the hundredfold. Before you can move on to something higher you must have perfect victory in your present position. The 'old man' tries to get victory in a place where he is not situated. You must get victory where you are. Only those who have walked it know the joy of a life of faith. In a battle, what counts is that you have had victory all along.

***

And truly our fellowship is with the Father and with his Son, Jesus Christ.   1 John 1.3

How can we enter the 'holiest of all', when the High

Priest only entered once a year? This has been taken too lightly. God's presence has not changed, his holiness has not changed, but the Holy Spirit brings us into his own fellowship, the fellowship of the Trinity. God has given me much over the years, gifts and estates, but they are as nothing compared with my fellowship with him. When you come into his realm, you are released from earthly things and your work from then on is to do the will of God. He in you will put more value on the things of eternity than on anything else. He will take the victories of the Saviour and apply them through you. At first your fallen reason cannot believe God, and he must change you. Faith will not follow human reason but reason will always follow faith. I think of my years of abiding. What a wonderful life it was to live 'within the veil' day after day. Self cannot abide in the Saviour, but as the Holy Spirit deals with you, he takes all the unbelief out of you. While you abide in the vine, all his life will flow through you. Everything of nature is to be subdued to the life of the Holy Spirit in you.

4

Rees Howells and Intercession

Intercession, as Rees Howells taught it, goes much further than prayer, because it operates at a deeper level. He never undervalued prayer, in fact to him prayer always meant answer and he would never lightly undertake it, only when the Holy Spirit gave him liberty to do so. Through prayer and the study of the Word of God he came to know the vital importance of faith. He faced the challenges to faith in the Bible with a firm belief, reinforced by years of experience, that the Bible means what it says and can be proved today, whether on a personal level or in national and international affairs. Throughout his life, as a young miner in a South Wales village, as a minister of the Gospel, as a missionary in Africa, and as founder and director of the Bible College of Wales in Swansea, he proved that the Bible is trustworthy and he expected God to work today as he did in times past. Along with his ministry of Intercession, he maintained to the end a personal life of prayer and faith.

From his early experiences in the village he found that there were situations that did not always yield to prayer. In some cases the devil was so deeply entrenched in a human life that prayer seemed unavailing. It was this that led Rees Howells, step by step, to discover the principles of Intercession and to obtain victory in each case. It led him into a path that perhaps few have trod, but he declared himself to be a 'pathfinder', a discoverer of the secrets of Intercession that enabled the men of the Bible to get victory.

Two things he always insisted upon: only the Holy Spirit can guide the intercessor in the path he must walk, and there must be faith equal to the intercession. He invariably warned against copying what the Holy Spirit had led him to do. Because he was led into strange and costly paths it might be thought that every intercessor must go that way. Rees Howells faced up to the challenge of the great intercessors of the Bible, men like Moses, Daniel and Ezekiel, whose intercessions operated in the affairs of nations. When, therefore, the Holy Spirit gave him the World Vision and he saw it attacked by the enemy through the dictators, Hitler, Mussolini, Stalin, he threw himself into the battle to secure freedom for the Gospel. To that conflict he brought all his years of experience in intercession, and continually the Holy Spirit gave him fresh light on the lives of the Bible characters and encouraged him to believe that God can work today with the same power.

However, the principles of Intercession can be demonstrated on any level and in any situation where the enemy appears to be in an impregnable position. Rees Howells used to say that the Holy Spirit is always original and so the pattern of Intercession will vary although the basic principles remain. The following may help to clarify some of these principles.

Some Principles of Intercession

1. Most fundamental of all is the principle that Intercession is based on the victory of the Lord Jesus Christ in his atoning death and resurrection. Where the enemy contests in a situation, and whatever may be the assault upon the intercessor, the victory will ultimately come through faith in the supreme sacrifice and glorious triumph of our Lord.

    Rees Howells used to say that as the Holy Spirit is the only actual witness on earth today of Calvary and the Resurrection, he therefore is the only person who can guide the intercessor along the path leading to victory. He also maintained that fundamentally there are only two Intercessors, the Lord Jesus Christ and the Holy Spirit.

    Wherefore he is able to save them to the uttermost that come unto God by him, seeing he ever liveth

to make intercession for them.   Hebrews 7.25
Likewise the Spirit also helpeth our infirmities: for
we know not what we should pray for as we ought:
but the Spirit itself maketh intercession for us with
groanings which cannot be uttered.
And he that searcheth the hearts knoweth what is
the mind of the Spirit because he maketh inter-
cession for the saints according to the will of God.
Romans 8.26, 27

It is the Holy Spirit therefore who must lead the intercessor and demonstrate through him the victory of Christ.

2. The New Testament makes it clear that there is a constant
   warfare going on in the heavenlies, and the apostle Paul,
   who knew this warfare well, was constantly urging his
   Christian converts to be aware of this, to be clothed with
   the heavenly armour and to 'fight the good fight of faith'.
   See Ephesians 6.10–18, 2 Timothy 2.1–5, 1 Timothy 6.12.

3. There is nothing automatic in this conflict. We see Daniel
   praying through for the fulfilment of the prophecy of
   Jeremiah concerning the return of the Jews to Jerusalem
   after the 70 years of captivity. If this could just be
   'claimed', why did he have to set himself to come before
   God with sackcloth, fasting and ashes? His prayer in
   Daniel 9 is the very model of the prayer of the intercessor.
   He identified himself with his people in their sin and besought the Lord, for his own sake, to remember his Word,
   to forgive and to restore.

   This same principle of identification can be seen also in
   the prayers of Ezra (chapter 9), and of Nehemiah,
   (chapter 1).

4. There are times when the intercessor finds himself up
   against very real forces, the principalities and powers, and
   the rulers of the darkness of this world (Ephesians 6. 12)
   who oppose the prayer. Here the Holy Spirit must guide
   the intercessor, as he alone knows the way to break

through the opposition. To any student of military history it is interesting to note how close sometimes is the parallel between the devices of earthly combatants and those of the spiritual foe.

5. A vital aspect of this spiritual conflict is that of the responsibility of the intercessor, once the Holy Spirit has called him to it. This is seen in the intercession of a man like the prophet Ezekiel, upon whom the Lord put bands which he dared not break. Whatever the cost the intercession must be carried out to the end. Why the cost? There are depths in this and a mystery which the Lord does not always choose to unveil. An intercession may at times have to be walked blind but ultimately the Holy Spirit will lead to a full realisation of victory. The intercessor knows then that he is 'through' and is given the complete assurance of victory. Then, sooner or later the victory will be manifested and there will be an outcome.

An illustration of this may be given from personal experience. The Holy Spirit called the intercessor to devote a week of prayer for a situation in a Christian group where forces were interlocked and something had to give way if the glory of God was to be upheld and his work maintained. The Holy Spirit himself, in a very clear and definite way, led the intercessor who was many miles away, to spend the week alone with God, and to be responsible to pray the situation through. Day after day the Scriptures were searched, and the hours spent with the Lord, and day after day there was a very real sense that the battle in the spirit was joined. It was suddenly on the fifth day that the Holy Spirit came upon the person concerned in an intense agony of soul. It was complete identification with the agony of one person vitally concerned in the situation and at the identical time when the crisis came to a head. After about an hour there was a sudden release in the spirit, a 'coming through' to an experience of complete victory and there was an overwhelming sense that the Lord had triumphed and his will and purpose had been fulfilled. Further prayer was impossible, only a spirit of worship and praise, a certainty that 'the Lord hath triumphed gloriously'. It was just three days later that news came that the victory had indeed been won, and in the years that followed the victory was worked out in wonderful ways.

6. The example given above demonstrates the power of intercession as exercised in a particular situation. Rees Howells also showed that intercession can apply in the work God gives to his servants, a work for which he makes them responsible. We might think of Hudson Taylor and the China Inland Mission, or Amy Carmichael and the work in Dohnavur, India. Such servants of God are totally committed to the work God has given them, knowing that whatever the burden and the difficulties they are responsible to continue; others may give up but they cannot. Anyone engaged in Christian work at any level will find it assaulted from within and from without. The enemy has many weapons in his armoury and will bring all his forces against a work of God. The one responsible must steadily persevere and hold on until victory comes in each test. The enemy will do everything possible to weaken faith, to undermine relationships, but as the intercessor finds comfort and strength in the Word of God and maintains faith in God amid all the attacks, the victory comes.

    In our own work also Rees Howells showed that those who, at a great cost to themselves, obeyed God's will and instead of going out to the mission field remained behind to serve him, perhaps in a very ordinary capacity, in college or school, were intercessors for those on the field and had a claim for the winning of souls in far countries.

7. It becomes abundantly clear that the path of the intercessor is the way of the Cross, but it is also the way of fellowship with Christ on a very deep level. Calvary was the supreme sacrifice of Love, and fellowship with the Lord in intercession leads to an ever-deepening realisation of, and entering into, this Love. Without love, as the

53

apostle Paul states in 1 Corinthians 13, 'it profiteth nothing'. The intercessor has 'the sentence of death' in himself (2 Corinthians 1.9) but as the dealings of the Holy Spirit are accepted and his leading obeyed, so the intercessor is led into a deep realisation of his identification with the Lord Jesus and an ever closer union with him. Truly, 'death worketh in us, but life in you' (2 Corinthians 4.12).

One of the early Christian leaders, afterwards martyred, said, 'My love is crucified', and as the intercessor is led into deeper paths of intercession, so he experiences more and more fellowship with the one who was Love Crucified. Down the centuries of Christian experience there have always been those, in differing walks of life and different callings, who have entered into this fellowship and union, who have come to know that God is Love and that this Love reaches out to a lost world.

Deeper Intercession

The Holy Spirit led Rees Howells into a realm of Intercession where few have penetrated, a realm beyond prayer, a realm of total commitment to the will of God and to complete separation from the things of the world, where the intercessor enters directly into the heavenly warfare between God and the devil, but where the victory of Calvary is proved wherever the enemy attacks in human affairs.

Jesus said, 'All power is given unto me in heaven and in earth' (Matthew 28.18), and he told his disciples to 'tarry in the city of Jerusalem' until they were 'endued with power from on high' (Luke 24.29). Only the Holy Spirit himself can lead the intercessor into that realm where the basic conflict between God and the enemy actually operates, and make him responsible to see the intercession through until God's purpose in it is achieved.

From the first simple prayer for which the Holy Spirit made him responsible, the prayer for the young man in the tin mill, Rees Howells was led into a deeper and deeper fellowship with the Saviour, being made more and more, 'conformable unto his death' (Philippians 3.10), yet in every test proving the power of the atonement and the Resurrection of the Lord Jesus, and experiencing in abundance the joy of the intercessor as he sees souls released from the power of the enemy.

5

The Village Years: Part One

It was in the village, an industrial mining centre in South Wales, that the Holy Spirit led Rees Howells to follow the Saviour through deep paths of humiliation, misunderstanding and suffering, but always he was brought out into wonderful victory and closer fellowship with the Lord. Not all are led in the way he was led, but it was in the village that he learned by experience the laws and principles of Intercession.

Preaching, by itself, did not touch a place which the great Welsh revival of 1904–6 had passed by, a place where poverty, sin, drunkenness and disease prevailed, and where Rees Howells saw souls bound by the devil, helpless to free themselves. He always said that until the Holy Spirit came into his life the devil as a person was never real to him, but from that time it was his main aim to 'bind the strong man' and steal his goods (Matthew 12.29), demonstrating the power of the atonement for sinners, however low they had fallen.

It was at this period of his life also that Rees Howells became established in a life of faith, learning to trust God daily, not only for his own needs but for those of many others. In finance, as well as in the winning of souls, he proved that 'faith is the victory'. One principle became firmly established in his mind, a principle that he proved repeatedly, that in the spiritual realm death must always lead to resurrection. He often quoted the words of our Lord in John 12.24, 'Except a corn of wheat fall into the ground and die, it abideth alone: but if it die, it bringeth forth much fruit.' He always claimed the victory in his intercessions, and in the sphere of finance this was especially the 'law of the hundred-fold'. He believed absolutely in the Saviour's promise of the hundredfold for all that is forsaken for his sake, and he proved its truth over and over again. He always emphasised that Intercession would not work without the faith equal to it, to put it through.

Guidance on Intercession

For as the sufferings of Christ abound in us, so our consolation also aboundeth by Christ.   2 Corinthians 1.5
Who now rejoice in my sufferings for you, and fill up that which is behind of the afflictions of Christ. Colossians 1.24

There are sufferings still left for the Church, to be fulfilled in us, but you cannot come to Christ's sufferings until you have finished with your own. The 'afflictions of Christ' are the afflictions of the kingdom and he is afflicted with us in them. As Isaiah said, 'in all their afflictions he was afflicted and the angel of his presence saved them' (Isaiah 63.9). In my intercessions I never once thought that he would allow me to suffer anything that he did not suffer with me.

There is a great difference between self-affliction and affliction for the sake of others. The sufferings of Christ are the sweetest thing on earth. The apostle Paul told the Colossians that he rejoiced in his sufferings for their sake, and his word to the Philippian church was 'that I may know him, and the power of his resurrection, and the fellowship of his sufferings, being made conformable unto his death (Philippians 3.10). This is intercession.

Likewise also the Spirit helpeth our infirmities: for we know not what we should pray for as we ought: but the Spirit itself maketh intercession for us with groanings which cannot be uttered.   Romans 8.26

In intercession you must always allow the Holy Spirit to direct you in it. Everything of yourself, of your own life, must go if you are to be an intercessor, but you cannot give your life for others if it belongs to you. There are only two Intercessors, the Saviour and the Holy Spirit, and the Holy Spirit must have a body to pray and intercede through.

I have never done one thing in intercession without his telling me. Before God can disclose his will to you, you must be willing for his will to be done through you and to pay the price. The strength of an intercession is the price paid for it. The Saviour placed the highest value on lost souls so that he was prepared even to die for them. That is why one soul is worth more than all the things of the world put together. I have never lost the consciousness that I was bought with the blood of the Saviour, and if he, who was perfect, was made sin for me, I should regret it throughout eternity if I had been unwilling for the Holy Spirit to pay any price through me for others. Many have accepted the gift of eternal life, but instead of realising that their life belongs to the one who died for it, they keep it to themselves. They are like the man in the parable who hid his talent in the earth instead of gaining on it.

For God so loved the world that he gave his only begotten Son, that whosoever believeth in him should not perish, but have everlasting life.   John 3.16

God has never changed his love, the love that was manifested in the Saviour on Calvary. This is the first condition in intercession, and the beginning of the life of the intercessor – to love enough to take the place of others.

One of the first things the Holy Spirit said to me at the convention, after he came in was, 'Of all the Father has given you, see that you lose nothing.' In this way he got me to pray only those prayers that he gave me and I was to be responsible for the answer. The first prayer he prayed through me was for a young man who was an outcast, who had not been home for two years and used to sleep on the boilers in the tin mill. When I went home I went to look for this young man. I used to walk through the village with him and I made him my companion and I am positive that the love I had for him was the love of the father for the prodigal son. The Holy Spirit took me right out of the company of other believers and gave me joy in this one soul. I prayed for him to have a blessing at Christmas and this was the first time I knew I had reached the throne and would get an answer. I saw the Saviour following one soul, the Good Shepherd who was bent on finding the sheep that was lost. There was something about this first soul that I had that caused me to know the joy of the Saviour, the joy of a soul brought out of death into life. I remember the day when he was dressed respectably and in chapel and when he went to London to see his mother.

Only the Saviour knows the value of a soul, and unless you have seen heaven and hell you do not know it. I followed this young man with the love of the Saviour, and if there is so much joy for one, what will it be when the harvest is gathered in!

———————◆———————

Thou shalt love the Lord thy God with all thy heart . . . and thy neighbour as thyself.   Mark 12.30, 31

One day the Holy Spirit showed me a village where there were many desperately needy people, drunkards, down-and-outs and such like, and he said, 'I want you to prove my love to these people so you must be the first sufferer.' This meant that whenever anyone was in need, I was to be willing to deprive myself first before any of them went without. The village was the first responsibility the Holy Spirit gave me and I became more responsible for the people there than my father was for our family at home. I know what it is to have a father's love because I am a father, but the love I had for the people in the village was more that that. I became a father to them and their sufferings became my sufferings. My father lavished his love upon us at home but his love was natural and therefore limited, but mine was God's love through me, the love that went to death on Calvary for lost souls, the love that has no limitations.

Every person who was in need I allowed him to supply it through me. They were blood-bought souls and I saw them as such. I proved to the full the joy of giving and the more I gave the more I wanted to give. When a strike threatened I was prepared to take credit at two shops so that they all could have essentials, and I was prepared to take on a liability up to £100. As the apostle Paul said, 'You may have many teachers but not many fathers.' I convinced these people with facts, not by talk.

———————————

There is no man that hath left house, or brethren, or sisters, or father, or mother, or wife, or children, or lands, for my sake and the gospel's, but he shall receive an hundredfold now in this time. Mark 10.29, 30

The first thing the Holy Spirit dealt with me on was my

money. He said, 'Do not pray one prayer for money until I have finished with all the money you have.' I never once interfered with his giving through me and he never limited his giving. He loved those people in the village with a father's love for his child, and I never knew him to give sparingly. He said, 'Remember, whatever you give up there is the hundredfold for it.' I was to invest on the hundredfold and this was the first place where I got victory over the enemy. I knew all the time that when I went to my extremity I would get the hundredfold. George Muller of Bristol knew well this law of giving and investing in the kingdom and then claiming the hundredfold.

I had to die to it first before the possession of money went out of me, but in the end I lost the world where money was current. I came to the place where I could be the same without a penny as I could with money in the bank. I thought, 'If he strips me of money, will I have equal victory in trusting God for my daily needs?' It is wonderful to walk with God and know that he will deliver you, and to the point I have given, I can prevail on God to move others to give. It works on laws.

It is not in the nature of man to give – it is of the Divine Nature. My first abiding in the village was, 'Give to everyman that asketh of thee . . . do good and lend, hoping for nothing again: and your reward shall be great, and ye shall be the children of the Highest: for he is kind unto the unthankful and to the evil.' (Luke 6.30. 35). Whoever would be in need, they had a claim on me and I found it more blessed to give than to receive, and the more I gave the more I wanted to give. I was tested on it for four years and never failed once. You would think the day would come when I should not be able to give, but there was the promise of the hundredfold for all that I gave, and I believed it. I had never once been without money for fifteen years, so could the Holy

Spirit make the promises of God equal to current coin?
When I got to the last pound the Lord said, 'Cut the
ropes and take the promises.'

---

*He that giveth to the poor shall not lack. Proverbs
28.27*

The first big test on giving came with a man in very
poor circumstances, the lowest of the low before he was
converted. One morning the Lord laid a burden on me
for him and told me to pray for him because he was in
difficulties. The devil was attacking him and I saw that
a contest was going on for his soul. It was a very keen
spiritual fight. I told the Lord, 'I will give all I have to
save him.' That evening the man came to see me, and
when I asked him if he was in trouble he said that he
was two years behind with his rent. 'Oh,' I said, 'I will
give you half of what you need and I am sure my friend
would like to give you the other half.' On my way upstairs to fetch the money the Lord spoke to me, 'What
did you say to him? I thought you said this morning
that you would give all you had.' I turned back and told
the man I would give him all he needed. Then I walked
back with him to his home. When I left him it seemed
that all the joy of heaven came down on me. It came
over me in waves, and I could not contain it. That night
I changed in the root of my nature. I changed towards
the world, towards lost souls and towards giving. From
that time I could not help but give to everyone in need. I
lived to give.

---

*Is not this the fast that I have chosen? . . . Is it not to
deal thy bread to the hungry and that thou bring the*

poor that are cast out to thy house? When thou seest the naked that thou cover him; and that thou hide not thyself from thine own flesh?   Isaiah 58.6, 7

When the Holy Spirit asked me to love every tramp on the road it was not I who really became responsible for them but God. He said, 'You do to them what the father did to his prodigal son in the parable.' I knew well what that father did; I had preached on it many times! The Lord said, 'I died for each one of these, and when you love as I love, you will be willing even to die for them.' Only the Holy Spirit could do that. Certainly I could give money to them but he wanted to make intercessions for them. The night after he spoke to me about them, there was a tramp in the meeting in the mission for the first time. Not one had come before this, but now they came, one after another, until at one time there were sixteen, including a family of four. My friend and I helped them, found lodgings and work for them, but then they started coming to my home and the Lord told me I was not to take a place at home that my family would not give them. I realised then that the position was going to be tested. It came when my brothers complained that the tramps showed no respect for my father and usually seated themselves in his chair. They also feared that some harm might come to my mother through them. My father knew that if he turned the tramps out, I would walk out that instant and he stood on my side. He said, 'You all bring your friends to the house and if Rees has sunk so low that he only has tramps for his friends, they must be free to come too.' The test had lasted for months but after this not one tramp came to my home. The test was not between the tramps and my parents but between natural love and spiritual love.

Seek ye first the kingdom of God and his righteousness; and all these things shall be added unto you. Matthew 6.33

The Word says, 'Sin shall not have dominion over you' (Romans 6.14), and unbelief is the greatest sin. Unbelief limits God and you cannot live a life of faith if you cannot trust him. Many people say, 'Oh, God is the owner of the silver and the gold,' but yet they cannot trust him. When he told me to love the tramps and help them, my first thought was, 'Why didn't he ask me while I had money?' But that would soon have finished in any case, but there was one source that would never fail – the unlimited resources of God. I was earning good money but I began to live on sixpence a day, on bread and cheese, in order to help the tramps and there were times when no one but God knew I needed money, and he used to send me what I needed to the penny. All the time I knew that the Holy Spirit in me was stronger than the enemy. It did not matter how many tramps the Holy Spirit brought: I knew that he was able to feed and clothe them all.

The best lesson I ever learned was that he could not answer me unless I had fulfilled the conditions. He wanted me to trust his Word, 'Take no thought for the morrow,' and he showed me that if I doubted this I was doubting him. You don't know what faith you have until it is tested. The Lord guided me step by step and he said, 'If ye abide in me, and my words abide in you, ye shall ask what ye will, and it shall be done unto you' (John 15.7). Abiding in him became natural, and every thought was brought into captivity. When there were disappointments in the village, I was not affected by them. Nothing people did could change the love of the Holy Spirit for them. I think of my years of 'abiding' in the village. What a wonderful life it was –

'within the sacred veil' day after day. The Word says, 'If I regard iniquity in my heart the Lord will not hear me,' (Psalm 66.18) but also, 'No good thing will he withhold from them that walk uprightly' (Micah 2.7) and 'Lord, who shall abide in thy tabernacle? who shall dwell in thy holy hill? He that walketh uprightly and worketh righteousness.' (Psalm 15.1, 2.)

If ye abide in me and my words abide in you ye shall ask what ye will and it shall be done unto you.   John 15.7

After the man in the tin mill I had many converts, but there was a woman in the village I could not reach personally, and the Holy Spirit asked me, 'Is it really necessary for you to come in touch with people in order to reach them? I want you to reach this woman by way of the throne, and to see that she is in the kingdom by Christmas Day.' To draw a soul into the kingdom without getting in touch with her was quite new to me. Could I bind the devil and take a soul out of his hands? She was said to be the worst woman in the village, really in his power. The Holy Spirit said, 'If you will allow me to bring you to a place of abiding, night after night, you can put this soul through on Christmas Day.' I used to go before him every night, with the Word, and I was not to go before him the next night until I had done what he told me. Everything in me that was not in accordance with his nature was to be taken out of me. Everything short of giving my life was tested, and he stripped me of things I never knew were in me, until I lived for one thing, the soul of this woman. In six weeks I had the witness that the victory was won, and then she began to come to the open-air meetings. I thought, 'Will she hold out until Christmas Day?' I was watching myself.

Could there be a doubt if there was no weakness in the abiding? God will never break a law to put you through. That is the abiding – taking all the unbelief out of you and binding the devil. On Christmas evening she was there in the meeting and down she went on her knees before the Cross. I told the devil, 'You are conquered.'

I am the vine, ye are the branches: he that abideth in me and I in him, the same bringeth forth much fruit.   John 15.5

One night there was to be a big meeting in the mission and my friend was due to come with me and take part. At six o'clock he sent to say that he was unable to come and I knew that I had depended more on him than on the Holy Spirit. Could I go back and ask him for his help when I had been depending more on my friend? During the two-mile walk to the mission I said to the Holy Spirit, 'I shall never let that happen again, and as a proof of my repentance, if you will come with me to this meeting, whatever you ask of me, when I come back this way, I will vow to you, like Jephtha, that I will give it to you tonight.' If ever the Lord was with me it was that night in the meeting, and as I was walking back I said, 'If there is anything in my life, or any position you want me to come to, I will give that to you tonight.' He said, 'There is a position I would like you to come to – to be a steward and not an owner of your money after tonight. You will only be able to give again as I tell you, because the money will be mine. Give the claim on your money to me.' I said, 'But my money is yours now.' He said, 'Yes, but when you want to give a gift you can give it; but now I want you to give up the ownership of your money to me.'

I had had such joy in giving, and I had lived in that joy for two years. Now he was going to take that away from me. Since he had made that change in my nature I had lived only to give, and the joy of the people I helped followed me. He said, 'After tonight you are not to give to anyone unless I tell you, and you are not to spend one penny except on necessities and essentials. The world is my parish and while there is one person without the necessities of life you are not to spend one penny on anything else.' I was earning money at the time and sacrificing in food and so on, but from that time I was only to give again as he would tell me. There and then I knelt down and called the stars and the Cloud of Witnesses to witness that henceforth I would not spend one penny except on necessities and essentials. At once the enemy said, 'Do you know what you have done? You are worse off than the people in Swansea prison.' I said, 'Yes, but I have done it by choice.' As soon as I said it, the whole heaven seemed to be illuminated, and the Holy Spirit said, 'Let me tell you what you have done. Tonight I have grafted you into the vine and you have become a branch in the vine.' It is not the branch that gets the fruit but the needy, and the vine can only produce the fruit through the branch. I saw myself as the medium between the Risen Lord and the world. The Saviour is in heaven and he can only give to the world through the sons of men. The realisation of it was almost unbearable. I became as dead to money as is a dead man and not once has God ever told me that I wasted his money. It was not that I learned to be content; no, I did not want it. I went out of the world where money was current. Could God have opened his treasury to a clearer channel to run his resources through?

6

The Village Years: Part Two

The Case of the Consumptive Woman

The challenge to lay down his life in an actual way for this woman led Rees Howells into a crisis experience which to him marked the real beginning of his life as an intercessor. All the previous dealings of the Holy Spirit with him in the village led up to this. The words of the apostle Paul in Galatians 2.20, were literally fulfilled in his life: 'I am crucified with Christ: nevertheless I live; yet not I, but Christ liveth in me; and the life which I now live in the flesh I live by the faith of the Son of God, who loved me and gave himself for me.' As he stepped into what was always to him a real death, the glory of 'the other side' was so great that it was difficult for him to come down to earth again for a considerable time. Again he could say with the apostle Paul, 'I knew a man in Christ . . . (whether in the body, I cannot tell, or whether out of the body, I cannot tell: God knoweth:) such an one caught up to the third heaven' (2 Corinthians 12.2, 3).

From this time the Holy Spirit had a new grip on his life and could command the absolute obedience necessary for his future paths of intercession. Deeper and deeper he was led into the sufferings of the world, but always proving that wherever the enemy of souls had brought men and women into any kind of bondage, the Saviour, in his death and Resurrection, could bring liberty and release.

Why did the Holy Spirit lead him into such personal suffering and deprivation? Here we touch that realm of warfare in the spirit that needs the faith of God himself to go through and get victory. In entering enemy territory, how can the intercessor prevail if he is still bound in any way by the enemy? He must be delivered from the law of sin and death into the law of the spirit of life in Christ Jesus (Romans 8.2). The Holy Spirit dealt drastically with the inner life of Rees Howells in order that he might become a clear channel for God to work through. He often referred to this 'change of his nature', and the ways in which the Holy Spirit dealt with him in various aspects of his natural life.

Abiding

This, to Rees Howells, was always the special path the Holy Spirit led him in a particular intercession. It could last weeks or months, involving difficult obediences and sometimes intense suffering, as he became more and more identified with those for whom the intercession was being made, but invariably resulting in a victory and joy that perhaps only the intercessor can experience.

Always bearing about in the body the dying of the Lord Jesus that the life also of Jesus might be made manifest in our body . . . So then death worketh in us but life in you . . .   2 Corinthians 4.20, 12

When I was born again it was only my own life I was living, and always rejoicing in my salvation. The Holy Spirit said, 'If you will allow me to come in I will take out the natural life, the life of the Fall, in you and replace it with the spiritual.' I went through this process bit by bit in the village after he came in: it was dying daily. It was not that he found fault with me but he was changing my nature. If the Holy Spirit is fighting the devil he must have a clear channel, and then, when the devil also has found a channel, there is a straight fight between the two. The Saviour had his own prepared body in which to make the atonement, but the Holy Spirit had to use a body affected by the Fall. He began to change me from self to others, and it was not a temporary change: I could not change back.

I am come that they might have life, and that they might have it more abundantly.   John 10.10

The difference between the Saviour and everyone who came before him was that he came to give life, but it was a life that could only come through death, his own death on Calvary. He was fulfilling a law which operates in spiritual things as well as in nature. 'Except a corn of wheat fall into the ground and die, it abideth alone: but if it die, it bringeth forth much fruit' (John 12.24). That is the way that the Holy Spirit has gained his intercessions in me, and it is on this principle he has worked. He showed me that he would put me on the Cross but that there would be resurrection on the hundredfold. It is just to the extent that you allow him to put you to death that his resurrection life will be manifest in you: 'For if we have been planted together in the likeness of his death, we shall be also in the likeness of his resurrection' (Romans 6.5). This is the life which always has the victory over the enemy.

Greater love hath no man than this, that a man lay down his life for his friends.   John 15.13

When the case of the consumptive woman came, the Holy Spirit said that he would prove through me that this disease had been taken away in Calvary. I saw what the Saviour had done in the atonement, and yet the devil was dragging thousands down to a lost eternity through this sickness. The intercessor must take the place of the one prayed for, and for six months he led me through a path of abiding for her healing, dealing with my nature down to its roots, until I became willing for the Holy Spirit to put her consumption into my body. But the test came when he said, 'The result of consumption is an early death, and now death has come for this woman. Will you take death?' In all those months the thought of death had not come to my mind, and I said, 'I have done all you told me. Have you found any flaw in my abiding? If you allow her to die, where is my abiding of these months? How can I continue to believe in you?' He said, 'There is no flaw in your abiding, but now death has come. You were willing for me to put her consumption on you, but now, will you take death as well?' I could have been an intercessor for consumption but death! It had never dawned on me that he would put my life to death: I was not prepared for this and I could not go through that day. Until then I had not known what it was to lose the face of the Father, and I cried like the Saviour, 'My God, my God, why hast thou forsaken me?' How great was the darkness that night and next day, but the following night a voice came out of the darkness: 'You did not know that it was a privilege I offered you – a place among the martyrs.' That instant I saw them, those who by choice had given their lives for the Saviour. I saw them and I made the transaction. I stepped into death – and I found that there was no death there. I was walking a path of discovery and I found that to the person born of God there is no death. 'Our Saviour, Jesus Christ, who hath abolished death and hath brought life and immortality to light through the gospel' (2 Timothy 1.10). That Easter I can truly say that I nearly left the body. I went out into the woods and entered into heaven. I saw the earth as cursed and I did not want to live a single day down here. If you offered me a throne I would not take it. I had seen that city where there is no death and I expected to be taken there at once.

But the woman for whom I offered my life would on no account pray that I should be taken in her place, although she had four little children. She had the chance to have life but she refused it and that day her face was radiant, like an angel's. Those were days of heaven upon earth, but after several weeks the Holy Spirit said, 'I am not going to take you, but from this time your body will be mine. You cannot dictate to me if I use your body to live in the way John the Baptist lived. You are to be a living martyr.' If he had kept my life and used it, only myself would have benefitted, but if it was put to death he could bring forth fruit on the hundredfold. She died, in wonderful victory, but outwardly the prayer had failed. I never once defended the position, which I knew was gained, but at the woman's funeral the Spirit came on the crowds of people who had gathered for it and it was, just like a revival.

Yea, Lord, thou knowest that I love thee. He said unto him, Feed my lambs.   John 21.15

The woman I had offered my life for left four little children and the first intercession he gained in me after this was to become a father to the orphans. The Lord said, 'This woman died in your place and if she was alive she would be bound to those children for at least 21 years. Are you bound like that?' I saw 21 years of my life going and only living with four little ones that did not belong to me. Their father neglected them and then went away and left them. The Holy Spirit wanted to take my body and be a father through me to those little children. I said, 'You must change me so that they can become to me what my brother's children are to him.' I changed in a moment of time and I loved those children with the love of God and not the love of man. I was preparing to go and live with them and care for them, but then some relatives of their mother claimed them. But the position was gained and he in me was indeed a father to the fatherless.

———————•◆•———————

A father to the fatherless and a judge of the widow is God in his holy habitation.   Psalm 68.5

When an intercession has been gained, the Lord will always give a proof. The Saviour was put to death for our sins and raised again for our justification (Romans 4.25). The proof of his victory was that he rose from the dead. When I made intercession for the consumptives and that woman died, he himself was to uphold the position, not I myself. I knew that I had gained it, and if the sacrifice was acceptable to God it was God who was to defend it. One of the first cases I had after the death of the consumptive woman concerned the husband of a woman who had about ten children. Her husband was dying and she was in great distress. I believe I carried as much of a burden as she did and I shed many tears that day. But sympathy does not go very far and the Holy Spirit told me that unless the man recovered I would have to support the widow and her children. I knew that he in me was a father to the fatherless and a comforter to the widow, but the morning I visited the house, while the wife was upstairs, I heard a voice speaking to me, saying, 'He is not to die, he is to live.' I told this to the woman but she could not take it from me. As I was walking home the Lord said, 'You did not speak to her with that certainty you use when you really know.' I said, 'I never heard anything like this before,' and he replied, 'You could not have heard it before because it came from beyond death. Tell her again.' What victory over death! I knew that death could not take that man, there was no death there. I went back next morning and told the woman, 'If your husband dies I will support you and your children.' I was away for a few days but when I returned I heard that the man was better.

The next case was the wife of a man I had helped financially. She was at the point of death but I knew she would not die. Death was in the room but I was in perfect peace. I said to the husband, 'I tell you she will get well and now we are going to have a praise meeting.' We prayed together and from then on there was a change and she began to recover. Many times after that I heard that voice I had heard in the house of the dying man, and each time there was victory.

7

The Village Years: Part Three

From the time that the Holy Spirit took that final and
absolute control, Rees Howells was led into a period of much
more intensive intercession. A chain of events led him, under
the guidance of the Holy Spirit, to make a final break with all
home ties and to live apart, alone with God. Outwardly it
often seemed a path of failure, but in reality his fellowship
with the Lord was deepened and strengthened as he was being
prepared for the wider ministry of later years.

To understand some of the Lord's ways with him at this
time it must be remembered that social conventions at the
turn of the twentieth century were very different from those
of today. For instance, men of all classes wore hats or caps
out of doors as a matter of course, and not to do so put a
person beyond the pale socially, and to allow hair and beard
to grow untrimmed was the mark of a social outcast. All this
Rees Howells was required to do, that he might identify himself with the lowest, and die to the opinion of the world, to his
friends and especially to his own family. In all this, although
it involved many a struggle at first, the Holy Spirit brought
him through into wonderful victory, so that he could rejoice
in the Lord in the midst of the deepest deprivation and glory
in the triumph of the Saviour over all the power of the enemy
in human life. He entered into a deep personal experience of
the love of Christ, a relationship which he always spoke of as
'the Bride'. In later years, when release would come after
periods of stress and tension, he could always revert to this
relationship and be refreshed and renewed in the love of his
Lord.

A special period of testing came after he entered into the position of a 'steward' of his money. He was still working in the local mine, and had come to know a wealthy business man from London. They had met at the Llandrindod Wells Convention, and Mr Gossett, recognising the deep spirituality of the young miner, invited him to London and accepted his way of life, although at this time Rees Howells was eating only bread and cheese and never wore a hat, something which caused his host acute personal embarrassment in the streets. It was for Mr Gossett's son that Rees Howells undertook one of his costliest tests, that of becoming a modern Nazirite.

Through Mr Gossett Rees Howells was introduced to Lord Radstock on whom he made a great impression. Lord Radstock was greatly used of the Lord, especially in Tsarist Russia among the aristocracy. It was beoming obvious that Rees Howells was on the threshold of a great public ministry under the patronage of these men. But the Lord's time for this had not yet come and he was called to leave home and enter into deeper abidings and more costly intercessions. Release came eventually and he was called to train for the ministry and then to go to Africa as a missionary.

A number of friends, one in particular, had stood with Rees Howells through much of his ministry in the village, but not all could stand with him in his later testings. One person was always steadfast in her support of him, even when others abandoned his friendship. This was Miss Elizabeth Jones, who later became his wife and was a true helpmeet to him throughout his life.

Testing Times
Ye shall bring a sheaf of the first-fruits of your harvest unto the priest and he shall wave the sheaf before the Lord to be accepted for you.   Leviticus 23.10, 11
The first of the first-fruits of your land thou shalt bring into the house of the Lord thy God.   Exodus 23.19
Christ the first-fruits . . .   1 Corinthians 15.23

Through Mr Gossett I was introduced to Lord Radstock, who had had revivals all over the country and throughout Russia. He had never heard of Intercession, that you had to die to every gained position before you could apply it. I told him of the Saviour, that until he died he was not to reign. In divine healing I knew I had gained it with the consumptive woman, but she died and the case went to the altar because the first-fruits belong to God. I had to walk it as a failure although the Holy Spirit had witnessed to me that the position had been gained, and I had many cases of healing after that. Lord Radstock had never understood why his young daughter died although he had believed to the end in her healing. Over her dead body he had said, 'Though he slay me yet will I trust in him.' From that time he had many cases of healing.

If ye keep my commandments, ye shall abide in my love.   John 15.10

The first real test on stewardship came soon after, at Christmas, when Mr Gossett sent me two books, and the thought came to me, 'I will send him a nice New Year card', but the Holy Spirit said, 'A New Year card is not an essential.' I said, 'It will only cost a penny,' but he said, 'The amount is not the question, but the principle.' So I wrote to Mr Gossett thanking him for the books and explaining why I could not send him a card. He replied, with a gift, saying, 'I would not take all the New Year cards in the world in exchange for your letter. Last Sunday I read it to all the patients in Westminster Hospital, and said, "A position gained by grace." '

For we are made a spectacle unto the world, and to angels and to men.   1 Corinthians 4.9

Every night for three years I walked the two miles to the Mission and I walked it with the Holy Spirit. I kept my cap in my pocket because I was in the attitude of prayer throughout the walk, and what fellowship we had together. One Sunday morning the glory of God came down on me as I was praying, and then the Lord showed me that my place of abiding for the next intercession to which he had called me, was to be in the attitude of prayer all through the day. This meant that I could not wear a hat at all, and would have to walk through the town as well as to the Mission without a hat. There was no more glory that morning! How could I go through the town without a hat? What would people think, above all, what would my mother think? I delayed going out that Sunday evening as long as I could, but at last could delay it no longer. My mother was waiting for me at the door, as usual, with my hat, and I can never forget the effect on her when I told her that I was not wearing a hat. My fasting had always cost her, but this meant being a public spectacle. Whatever I was doing throughout the day I was to be in the attitude of prayer. It was a real death to go to work without my hat although in time people got used to it.

---

*The soul of Jonathan was knit with the soul of David, and Jonathan loved him as his own soul.   1 Samuel 18.1
Jonathan strengthened his hand in God. And he said unto him, 'Fear not . . . thou shalt be king in Israel and I shall be next unto thee.'   1 Samuel 23.16, 17*

The friend who always worked with me in the Mission

was a most lovable person and a wonderful speaker, especially in the open-air meetings. One night, when he had spoken before me, the thought came to me, 'How can I ever preach after that?' and a thought of jealousy entered. How the Holy Spirit dealt with me that night! He showed me what was in me and how this could be a hindrance to the people we were working for. He said, 'If you allow this to happen again I will have you to go on your knees in the open-air and confess it openly.' I knew he meant it and from that day on I never dared to cherish a thought of jealousy.

The time came when people began to tell my friend that he would never have a real chance while he was with me and that he should have a work of his own. I knew that the enemy was attacking him and the Lord said, 'Give the leadership of the Mission over to him and be a real intercessor behind him. Pray that the Mission will be a greater success in his hands than in yours.' The Mission had been everything to me for three years and it took the Lord several days to get me through on this. But I gave the Mission to my friend and the Lord enabled me to love him with a real love although he took my place.

Hath the Lord as great delight in burnt offerings and sacrifices, as in obeying the voice of the Lord?   1 Samuel 15.22

These positions are gained inch by inch. My next place of abiding was to put a soul through who was at a distance from the village. I was to be on two meals a day of plain food and I was not to wear a hat. A week or two later I was invited up to London to spend a week with Mr Gossett, to meet Sir Robert Anderson and other leading Christians. The question was: should I break my abiding in order to mix with people like this? In my heart I thought to sacrifice the visit to London and I told the Lord, 'I would rather remain an intercessor than go to stay at Buckingham Palace.' I was living in a realm where God is and where all men are only mortal men to you. Then the Lord spoke to me, 'Can you not abide in London?' I said, 'Show me one man in the Bible who has done something like this.' He said, 'John the Baptist.' Not any money would have tempted me to betray Mr Gossett's kindness, but obedience to God would. I did not move from my abiding when I went to London, either in food or in wearing a hat, and I was the greatest blessing to Mr Gossett. It tested him to drive in an open cab with me, without my hat, from Paddington Station to Piccadilly, and he could not face walking through the streets with me like this, but he poured love and kindness on me. The Lord told me that he would make Mr Gossett's son the test case of my intercession and that Captain Gossett would not return to the army until he was a converted man. The Lord told me, 'You are going back for two years and after that I will use you for the world.'

All the days of the vow of his separation there shall no razor come upon his head . . . All the days of his separation he is holy unto the Lord.   Numbers 6.5, 8

When I returned from London the Lord said, 'If I should let you go free now there are places of intercession you have not yet gained.' If Joseph had been set free after he had interpreted the dreams of the butler and the baker, he would probably have returned home to his father, but because the Lord kept him in prison for two more years he came to the throne of Egypt. The

Lord said, 'If you will allow me to keep you alone with myself for another two years, the difference will be between Joseph going home and Joseph ruling Egypt.'

I was no longer to go to the Mission but I was to read the Word every night on my knees, from 6 p.m. until 9 p.m. and I was to obey him no matter what position of the prophets he called me to come up to. I came to Numbers 6.2–9. I was to be a Nazirite! He said, 'I have separated you for two years; you are not to touch the world for two years, neither is it to influence you.' It was not just a matter of a man not shaving, but I was to be holy, separated unto God. When he told me this I knew my parents would be tested but I was not to tell them why I was doing this. People would look after me on the street, and talk about me but I was not to open my mouth to a single person. I was not to touch the world in thought or mind, let alone action. The only picture that came to my mind was that of the first person I had helped, the man in the tin mill, the one it had cost me so much to walk with. I said to the Lord, 'The tramps were bad enough, but to be like a tramp myself, that would be the end of my parents.' He said, 'Put your parents on the Cross and tell me the real reason why you are not willing to be a Nazirite.' I said, 'The influence of the world will overcome me,' and he said, 'That is why I have called you to it, and you will be a Nazirite until you are dead to every thought of the world, and no person can exert any influence over you.'

People thought that something had gone wrong in London and that I had come back a disappointed man. I no longer went to the Mission in the evening; I did not go out at all on Sundays; I had only one suit of clothes and I was not shaving. It was evident that I had gone too far this time and that my mind was affected! Everything in me was to be tested and especially my relationship with my people. Daily I walked what my father was going through – the thoughts that would come to him – but I was to die to every thought of that. It was one of the worst deaths I ever walked, to become dead to my father's feelings and only alive to the feelings of the Saviour. Do you tell me that the Saviour never walked this, that his mother and his brothers would suffer? But during this time I was entering into the sufferings of the Saviour and I had a fellowship with him I never had before.

It took me two weeks to get the victory and become dead to the influence of the world, but before the end of six months, instead of the world influencing me it was I who was influencing the world. People sensed the presence of God with me and I brought them face to face with eternity. Some even took off their hats as they passed me on the street and one old man used to say, 'There goes a modern John the Baptist.' At the end of six months I came free and had the assurance that the intercession had been gained. I remember the night I came free and went to tell my mother. I can hear her now saying, 'Thank God you are through.'

It was some time after that Mr Gossett's son left the army and went to Canada where he had a farm, and both he and his wife were converted in a meeting held by an evangelist.

Heal the sick, cleanse the lepers, raise the dead, cast out devils: freely ye have received, freely give.   Matthew 10.8

The first case of healing I had in public was that of my uncle. When you tell people that you or God will do a certain thing that seems impossible, you are aware that the day will come when you will have to face it, and then it seems nearer to you than the dawn. One of the things I faced up to in the impossible was when the Holy Spirit said, 'In four and a half months your uncle will be healed.' He had been ill for 30 years and was someone with whom I had the most perfect fellowship. Everyone came to know about the prophecy of his healing, and when I passed people in the street it was this that always came to their minds. Unless you have done something like this you can only imagine it: days of waiting when you face the impossible and must prove that the God of the impossible is with you. How can you keep steady under it? The Lord had told my uncle that he would be healed on May 15, Whit-Sunday, and that he would be in the chapel that morning. About two weeks before the time, the Lord told me to leave home and go and live in rooms. I was to hide myself as Elijah did by the brook. Everyone thought that I had run away and left my uncle in the test. So once again people's attention was caught and I thought, 'Why does he have me to do this?' But he would take no arguments. I had plenty of time to think – 24 hours of the day – but we do not always know God's purpose or his will in a situation. I had invited two of my friends to have tea with me that day, but when they came they had no news of my uncle. A message had been sent to me but it was not delivered. Then the Holy Spirit told me that my best friend had not believed and that I was to speak to him next morning. If there was a thought of failure in my mind how could I rebuke him? He said, 'It was very difficult to believe.' The question was: had anyone believed it? I had hours alone with God that day until 11 o'clock at night, when some friends called and said, 'You are quite right. Your uncle was in chapel yesterday morning.' If I had doubted, could I have rejoiced?

Because for thy sake I have borne reproach: shame hath covered my face. I am become a stranger unto my brethren and an alien unto my mother's children. When I went and chastened my soul with fasting, that was to my reproach. I made sackcloth also my garment; and I became a proverb unto them . . . But as for me, my prayer is unto thee, O Lord, in an acceptable time.
Psalm 69.7, 8, 10, 11, 13

When the case of my uncle's healing came, the Lord told me that my people did not believe it and I was to leave home. This was worse than my other tests – to leave home of my own accord. What excuse could I give? If I had told my mother that she was not believing she could have said, 'How do you know that I do not believe?' Neither my father nor my mother had given me any cause to be offended. When I was dealing with the tramps and even when I became a Nazirite my mother had kept herself out of it entirely.

Before you come to this, every affection, every tender tie must be broken until the souls of other people become to you the same as the souls of your own people. I went down to my uncle and told him that I would be away from home until I had gained all my intercessions and I did not know when that would be. Although my uncle loved my mother, he did not say a word to her about it: the will of God was always first with us both. What a scene it was when I told my mother that night that I was leaving home. I know what the Saviour went through; his mother was in the crowd when he was crucified.

I was months away from home and everything in me by nature was to be subdued to the life of the Holy Spirit who was in me. I could see a very great meaning in it afterwards because my mother had found it difficult enough to accept my former fasting, but this was to be much greater. I lived in the same village as my parents but I was not to see them, and everybody thought that there was something between us. The Lord called me to intercede for the widows of India, to bind the devil who was causing their bondage. I slept on a plank and only ate one meal every two days – no bread, no food with any taste – just enough to keep body and soul together. At first it was agony, but before the intercession could be complete I would have to come to the place of not wanting to change the position. In ten days I got the victory and then I had no desire to change and I went on for ten weeks. He changed my taste and he changed my body. When he put me on one meal every three days, what a test it was to go from 48 hours to three days. It is not trying to do it oneself; it is the Holy Spirit who must do it. When he saw that I had victory in the three days, he began to deal with me about going 40 days, as Moses did, and the Saviour. I said, 'My body is yours – I will do it if you tell me.' I remember that morning when I told him, and it seemed all the angels of heaven were around me. He allowed me to go 15 days and then stopped me. He said, 'You have finished all.'

Your Father knoweth what things ye have need of, before ye ask him . . . Seek ye first the kingdom of God and his righteousness; and all these things shall be added unto you.   Matthew 6.8, 33

The day came when the Holy Spirit said, 'Why should you be giving seven hours a day of your time to an earthly master? Leave that now and come and work for me. Do you believe that I can keep you?' I was on the Black Mountain at the time and the Lord said, 'If you believe that I can keep you, put up your hand and tell me, "I shall not take from a thread to a shoe-latchet from any person unless the Lord tells me."' So as Abraham refused to take the spoils of war, I put up my hand and made the vow (Genesis 14.22, 23). He told me not to take a meal at home without paying for it and I said, 'I will go out as your earthly disciples did. Do not change for me the principle that you laid down for them.' (Matthew 10.9). I was not now active in the Mission or in contact with many people. My mother was unwilling for me to pay for my meals, but when I insisted that otherwise I would have to leave home she finally gave in. She had hoped that now I was going to live a normal life after the test of being a Nazirite. It was arranged that I would pay every month and I spent the first month alone on the mountain, alone with God, and what a wonderful month it was. The Lord had told me not to pray for money until the time came to pay at home.

When I went home my father said, 'The manager has kept your job open for you and you can take it again if you want to.' I said, 'Why should he do that?' My father said, 'If you don't mean to earn a living again who is to keep you?' I said, 'I am working for God and I believe that he can keep me.' He said, 'Can you name a single person who has lived this life before?' I said, 'George Muller.' He said, 'He is dead. Can't you name someone who is living?' I said, 'Do you believe the words of the Saviour, "Take neither purse nor scrip . . . the labourer is worthy of his hire." ' He said, 'I only brought you a message.' Just then a letter came from Mr Gossett offering me a post with the London City Mission at a salary of a £100 a year and he had underlined the words, 'Those who preach the Gospel should live of the Gospel.' My father was pleased but I said, 'Those who preach faith should live by faith.' My father laughed and within half an hour I was delivered of the very amount I needed. From that day to this I have never doubted that God would supply my needs. When my wife and I were married we lived from day to day for two years, and after that he called me to the ministry.

Thou shalt love thy neighbour as thyself.   Mark 12.31
Thou shalt not hate thy brother in thine heart . . .
Thou shalt not avenge nor bear any grudge against the
children of thy people.   Leviticus 19.17, 18

One of my early converts, Joe Evans, was in the last stages of consumption and the doctor advised him to go to a tropical country, but his parents were very poor. I was baffled at first when the Holy Spirit told me to follow the doctor's advice and also sent me £300. Madeira was decided upon, but who was to take him? A great future was beginning to open up for me. Would you attend to a consumptive in the last stages of the disease, and share his room? Was I willing to lose my health for the sake of Joe's healing? I was tested to the hilt but I gave up preparation for the ministry in order to take him to Madeira.

The cheaper of the two hotels was Portuguese but the food soon upset Joe so the Lord told me to let Joe go to the English hotel and live myself on 10d. a day. The English missionary offered me the *Sailor's Rest*, which was the basement of his mission house. This had not been occupied for months, except for numerous insects. My food was covered with them in the morning and this, along with everything else, seemed altogether too much. I began to have thoughts in my mind against the missionary, and as I nursed this feeling I wanted to cry. But the Holy Spirit said, 'Let me speak to you. Have you not preached on the way Ezekiel lived? Would you like me to put you on that instead of in the *Sailor's Rest*?' I asked the Lord to forgive me and he said, 'It is not that. I brought you to Madeira to show you that there was a position you had not come up to – loving those who do something against you.' I saw the difference between the Saviour and the way I was limiting the Holy Spirit in me. That day I went out to the hills of Madeira and worshipped the Saviour. I said, 'Don't let me free until you gain this in me.' The Saviour was 'wounded in the house of his friends' and I knew now that I had not gone to Madeira only so that my friend would be healed but for this change to be made in me. In six weeks I changed, and what a life I came into! Oh, that perfect love that was in me! Next day the evangelist asked me where I was living and I said, 'In the *Sailor's Rest*'. He said, 'Not in the house but in the *Sailor's Rest* ? Do you call that Christianity in your country?' I replied, 'Do you pay for your electric light or your laundry? That is what the missionary does for me.' What victory!

Soon after this Joe became very ill and wanted to go home to die. I said I could not do that: it would be the first defeat in my life. I said, 'Surely the Lord will speak to me,' and within an hour he did. He told me he had brought Joe to Madeira to go to the very end of the law of nature, but he would be healed within a month. A specialist who examined Joe said he was in a very critical condition and should go home. When I announced that Joe was to be healed the effect on everyone, including the missionary, was very great. Meanwhile I wrote home to say we would be back in a month's time and that Joe was to be restored. We would send a cable on the morning of the healing. Early that morning Joe came into my room and there was no change in him. The Lord said, 'Are you sending that cable?' I asked the cause of the delay and he said, 'If you take the healing from me against what you can see and what Joe says, you will have gained a higher position than in the healing of your uncle.' Within an hour I came through and sent the cable: 'Victory'. Next day the Lord came down on Joe like a shower of rain and he was healed on the spot. Two days later we left Madeira, and when we reached home Joe's doctor examined him and could find no trace of the disease. On the Sunday the doctor went to chapel for the first time since he had come to the district.

Marriage and Ministry

In his last months in the village Rees Howells had been separated from his former active life among the people and the Mission had been given over to his friend. After the experience in Madeira great changes were to take place in preparation for his future ministry. Soon after returning from Madeira, with Joe, he married Miss Elizabeth Hannah Jones, who had stood by him throughout the prolonged testings in the village, and together they lived a life of faith, trusting God daily for their needs. During a short visit to America he began to preach again, and when they returned home the Lord told him to attend services in the chapels again. He had had no connection with the local chapels for more than five years, but his spiritual power was soon recognised and the elders invited him to enter the ministry. The Lord had prepared him for this and he entered a theological college in Carmarthen, and later was ordained in the Congregational Church.

Mr and Mrs Howells first came in touch with missionary work in Africa through some missionary friends in Angola, Mr and Mrs Stober. They offered to care for their little girl while her parents were abroad, but the Stobers, although much touched by the offer, did not accept it. It was at a meeting during the annual Llandrindod Convention, when Mr Albert Head was speaking on behalf of the South Africa General Mission, that Mr and Mrs Howells felt the burden for Africa and then the call came to them both to go to the mission field.

8

Out from the Village

From a life of solitude, alone with God and his word, Rees Howells had been called to mingle again with people, to train for the ministry, and then to go to Africa as a missionary. But during those years in the village, reserves of spiritual power were built up which were to have a mighty outcome in later years, first in Africa and then in the Bible College in Swansea. During his time in the ministry he concentrated on preaching the New Birth as he felt that this was greatly needed in the chapels, some of which had not associated themselves with the preaching of the great Welsh Revival of 1904–6.

It was in Africa that he proved the power of the inter-cessions gained in the village, and in Africa that the Holy Spirit was poured out in 'rivers of living water'. The call to the mission field was preceded by perhaps the greatest inter-cession of all, an intercession that cost both Rees Howells and his wife to the depths. The Lord asked them, not just to leave their infant son, Samuel, behind, but to give up all future claim to him. In Africa they were to give their undivided attention to the winning of souls, and for this sacrifice Rees Howells claimed 10,000 souls in Africa; he was confident that he would get them and he did.

It was also in Africa that he again challenged death in the great influenza epidemic after World War One, and he proved the power of the Holy Spirit to break the bondage of certain heathen customs.

The Ministry

For I determined not to know anything among you, save Jesus Christ and him crucified.   1 Corinthians 2.2

When I went back to preaching in the chapels I preached the simple Gospel, and what a privilege it was to stand in the pulpit and share the unsearchable riches of Christ. There is no glory like that of proclaiming the Cross. I preached more on eternal life than on the person of the Holy Spirit, as many believe in the atonement and the Resurrection, but they have not the personal experience of passing from death unto life. The Lord allowed me to return to a most natural life again and I was always thankful that he gave me the privilege of preaching to the multitudes in many chapels in the district.

Now faith is the substance of things hoped for, the evidence of things not seen.   Hebrews 11.1

When I was in the ministerial school there was not much need of faith because I was preaching every Sunday, but when I was called to Africa the Lord told me to go to Livingstone College to take a course in medicine. There were expenses up to £100 and also my wife was in a Bible school. Where would the £100 come from? But it was the Lord who had told me to go there. I asked my cousin to sign the application form for me, and he asked whether I had the money. He would have given it to me himself if he had it at the time but I said I would not take it. 'When I go to London the Lord will give it to me.' I could see that I was speaking down deep to the soul of my cousin; the Holy Spirit speaks with authority. 'Are you quite sure you will be delivered?' he asked. 'Quite sure,' I said. I went to London with only a single fare and within a week I was delivered of the money.

For God so loved the world, that he gave his only begotten Son, that whosoever believeth in him should not perish, but have everlasting life.   John 3.16

My wife and I were to go to Africa and because we loved souls, the Lord made a very great test on it. He said, 'You must prove to me that you love the souls of those people in Africa, who are to live for eternity, more than you love your own son.' I thought, 'Does he really mean this?' Yes, he meant it, even as he had told Abraham to take his only son up a mountain and offer him for a burnt offering. There are men God has tested, and he tested me whether I loved anything in this world more than I loved souls. Everything has to be tested and to go through the fire. God knew that 2000 years after he asked Abraham to give up his son, he would have to do the same thing. 'He who spared not his own son but delivered him up for us all . . .' (Romans 8.32). And as Isaiah said, 'It pleased the Lord to bruise him' (Isaiah 53.10). Your love for God must be proved – he does not take your word for it. The acid test of our love for souls was Samuel. God said, 'If you give him up you can never claim him again.' Not once has it ever dawned on me that Samuel was mine. God had said to Abraham, 'In blessing I will bless thee,' and the one thing I told the Lord was, 'I can claim the hundredfold in souls from you in Africa.'

Bind the sacrifice with cords, even unto the horns of the altar.   Psalm 118.27

I gave Samuel up on a point of intercession, and he was never to be ours again. The Lord said, 'This is the price and you must pay it.' I had walked tests before but never anything like this. You may preach about God giving his son without being moved, but when you are called to give yours you are moved every time you see the name of the Son of God. How can you know what it cost God to give his only begotten son if you have the chance to give yours and you do not do it? We were not even to find a place for him, but my uncle and aunt sent for me. They had never seen Samuel but they said they were to take him; he was to be theirs entirely, and my sister was to be his nurse. I think in eternity we shall look back on what we went through the morning she came to take him. When he went, not only was the house emptied but our hearts were emptied too. I asked my wife that night how she had got through and she said that she had gone out into the garden to weep. The lines of a well-loved hymn came to her:

> But we never can prove the delights of his love
> Until all on the altar we lay.

Now she had to prove it. Then the Lord spoke to her: 'Measure it with Calvary.' She saw what the Father did with his son and she came through.
I never once interfered in Samuel's life. They changed his name and they planned his education. I have always referred to my uncle and aunt as his parents and I never claimed him as mine.

He that believeth on me, as the Scriptures hath said, out of him shall flow rivers of living water. (But this spake he of the Spirit which they that believe on him should receive.)   John 7.38, 39

When I went to Africa I knew I was taking the Holy Spirit there and that as soon as he would get a chance he would pour himself out on that place as he did at Pentecost on Jerusalem. I knew I had a claim on 10,000 souls because of the sacrifice we made of Samuel. Everything the Lord had told us to do we had done. The price had been paid and not the least was the giving up of Samuel. I never thought to do anything else in Africa but to win souls. The Saviour said that rivers of living water were to flow out of the one in whom the Holy Spirit was living, and I knew he was living in me. He also said, 'Bring ye all the tithes into the storehouse and prove me now . . . if I will not open you the windows of heaven and pour you out a blessing that there shall not be room enough to receive it' (Malachi: 3.10), and I had brought the tithes into the storehouse. He also told me to pray that he would give the Saviour 'the heathen for his inheritance' (Psalm 2.8). There was power even in telling this and I went to Africa to get those 10,000 souls.

And it shall come to pass in the last days, saith God, I will pour out of my Spirit upon all flesh.   Acts 2.17

When we arrived in Africa, the people asked us to tell them of the Welsh revival, and they wanted to know if we had brought that blessing with us. I said, 'Yes, we have.' The Africans had no word in their language for 'revival' because there had never been one in that part of the country. They asked me to preach to them on this and I told them how the Holy Spirit came down at Pentecost with almighty and divine power, and that the power came down not only on the disciples but on the people gathered in Jerusalem. They heard with amazement that the Holy Spirit even did away with the barrier of languages. I told them how the Holy Spirit came to dwell in my life and that if he entered them as he entered into Peter, there would be the same result. I also told them that as the apostle Paul met the Saviour on the way to Damascus, so I had met him, and that as he spoke to the apostle, so he spoke to me. As I preached on revival and what God had prophesied through Joel, I came to believe and expect it. I was expecting the heavens to be opened and the Holy Spirit to come down and those rivers of living water to flow.

And when they had prayed, the place was shaken where they were assembled together; and they were all filled with the Holy Ghost, and they spake the word of God with boldness.   Acts 4.31

People had worked on that mission station for seven years without a single convert. They had laid a wonderful foundation but when the Holy Spirit came, he swept hundreds into the kingdom. One Thursday evening, four of us were reading the Bible together and I said, 'The Holy Spirit is coming down in this district and will give a Pentecost.' I told them the prayer had been heard and there was no need to pray any longer. A few days before this we had begun to sing the chorus: 'Lord, send a revival, and let it begin in me.' Everywhere people were singing it and I knew the sound of it, a sound you cannot make, the sound of revival, something which brings you into the stillness of God. Every moment we were expecting him to come. The following Sunday was my birthday and I knew the day before that the Holy Spirit would come down on that day. It was in the afternoon that he came upon a young girl who broke down in tears as she prayed. Within five minutes the whole congregation fell on their knees, crying to God. The Holy Spirit came with power such as I had never seen, even in the Welsh Revival, and had only heard of through reading of men like Finney and others. The meeting went on late into the night and continued day after day from 9 o'clock in the morning until 6 o'clock in the evening, for seven days. We baptised 67 on the same day and great numbers after that. Everyone who called on the name of the Lord was saved and the revival lasted for 15 months without a break, with two revival meetings every day and meetings all day on Fridays. Evangelists were going out from the station all on fire for God and hundreds were converted.

For the waters were risen, waters to swim in, a river that could not be passed over . . . and everything shall live whither the river cometh.   Ezekiel 47.5, 9

All the other missionaries in the South Africa General Mission heard of the blessing in Rossitu and began to pray daily, between 7 and 7.30 a.m. for the Lord to pour out of his Spirit upon the other stations. Our people prayed also and I began to pray at 6 o'clock every morning, 'Lord, why don't you pour out your Spirit on these other mission stations?' After a month of praying, with great liberty, the morning came when I lost myself in God and I saw the Holy Spirit descending on Africa. As truly as John the Baptist saw the Holy Spirit coming down on the Saviour, I saw him coming down on all those mission stations, and he told me that as I had prayed and believed, he would send me to every place where the Spirit was to come down. I was overcome in his presence.

Not long afterwards a letter came from the Committee asking me to come to a conference at Durban. I was asked to take prayers and for three weeks I spoke morning and evening, and the Spirit came down and blessed everyone of the missionaries. On the last day of the Conference the chairman said, 'You have been a blessing to us and we want the people on all our mission stations to have the same blessing. It is only right that you should go to every one.' I spent a month alone with God and I had to go through every stage of believing. The enemy said, 'How will you carry the blessing from one state to another in South Africa, when the languages are not the same?' I said, 'I am carrying within me the source of all revival and there is no need for another to carry it.' We travelled throughout South Africa and in every place the Holy Spirit came down. There was not a single place where we did not prove Pentecost. At every mission station there was an open heaven. I laid my hands on thousands and every one came through. He never failed once. If the Holy Spirit is in you, can you believe for these living waters?

For this purpose the Son of God was manifested, that he might destroy the works of the devil.   1 John 3.8

The revival was continuing on our mission station but few of the married men were converted because of the custom of the Labola, by which men sold their daughters, often when they were very young. One young girl in our school was sold to a very wicked old man and she refused to live with him. Her father had spent the money paid for her and because she refused to leave home, he was arrested. If £20 were not paid, she would have to go to prison for two years and even then she would not be free. I was deeply touched, but what was the use of being touched unless you did something about it? Two policemen came to our school to arrest her. She had accepted the Saviour, and her chief concern was for her father. Others might condemn him but she would not. I told her that I would pay the money and release her. I shall never forget her look of relief and the effect all this made on the district.

The Lord asked me, 'Do you think I can break the power of the Labola?' I said, 'Certainly, you can.' If you give them the same blessing I had when I accepted the Saviour this will stop. He said, 'Test the intercession and break the power of the Labola.' I knew I had a position to pray against the power of the devil over a soul – to make the person free to make a choice of the Saviour. Six of the married men came to help to build my house and after about three months I asked them to come to a Sunday morning meeting. In the first meeting the leader of these six men was converted and finally five of the six were put through into the kingdom. It was the first breakthough but it was the test of the influenza that completed it.

Thou shalt not be afraid ... for the pestilence that walketh in darkness: nor for the destruction that wasteth at noon-day. A thousand shall fall at thy side, and ten thousand at thy right hand; but it shall not come nigh thee. Psalm 91.5–7

When the influenza came to Africa, hundreds were dying daily. Then it came to our mission station and in a few days we had 65 down with it. The Holy Spirit told me that although hundreds were dying around us, not one was to die on the mission station. It was not easy to believe this but the Lord inspired the believing in me and I trusted his word in Psalm 91. When I challenged death in the influenza, the chief came to know of it and he sent to ask me if I would attend to his people if they had this illness. When I told him that not one would die on the mission station it caused a great sensation. The chief then asked if his people could come up to the mission station to avoid death. God was taking advantage of the influenza to do what no one else could do. The witch doctors themselves were down with it and they said that because their ancestors had never had this sickness the ancestral spirits could not cope with it.

It went round a radius of about 20 miles that the God of the white man was able to keep death away. I wanted to prove that our God is a living God and greater than all the ancestral spirits. First to come were five of the most Gospel-hardened married men, with their wives carrying their sleeping mats, and then many more. The test lasted for over three months and I worked day and night on these people. My wife was very ill but I told her that she could not die, and I was greatly tested on two cases. I could not move their temperature but the Lord gave me the victory. There was not a single death, and so great was the victory that many were convicted and accepted the Saviour. After the epidemic was over one side of the chapel was full of married men.

Back to Wales

Returning home, ostensibly on furlough, in 1920, Rees Howells preached with tremendous power in churches and conventions. In the Llandrindod Convention of 1922, when the appeal was made for full surrender, the whole audience rose to its feet. The way was opening for a worldwide ministry as a revivalist, and the Council of the Mission made him a free lance, asking him to take five years to travel all over the English-speaking world, as the Holy Spirit led him. But once again God crossed his path and once again he was called to an entirely new experience, one which was to involve a period of seclusion again and months of testing and great trials and triumphs of faith.

The Lord told him that he was to found and establish a Bible college so that young people might come to learn a life of faith and above all be filled with the Holy Spirit. So once more 'the corn of wheat' had to fall into the ground in order that the power of God might be released in the lives of others.

The full story of the revivals in Africa is given in the book *Rees Howells, Intercessor* by Norman Grubb. In it he also tells how the Bible College of Wales in Swansea came into being and was opened in 1924. The twenty-six years that followed were the final chapter in the life and ministry of Rees Howells.

9

Great Intercessors of the Bible

Through his grasp of the principles of Intercession, Rees Howells had great insight into the lives of the great intercessors of the Bible, men and women who were prepared for any sacrifice, even to life itself, so that God's glory might be upheld and his purposes for their nation fulfilled. In every test he sought strength and inspiration from the light the Holy Spirit shed on the lives of these and other great Bible characters.

The months he had spent alone with God and the Word, together with the path along which the Holy Spirit led him in personal experience, gave his teaching unusual depth and inspiration. Long after his village days, the years in the ministry and as a missionary, he continued to be a man of mainly one book, and to receive light on the lives of men like Moses, Ezekiel, Daniel and others. When he founded the Bible College of Wales, in Swansea, this light was frequently transmitted to staff and students, who were often awed and spellbound in college meetings as light from heaven came on the Word. Over and over again the stillness of eternity settled on the meeting; the majesty and holiness of the Almighty were revealed and his presence pervaded the hall. The need for man to have a mediator and intercessor became intensely real, and the depths through which Jehovah led a man such as Moses, in the days before the Son of God came to this earth and made the supreme atonement, were better understood. His own early experiences in the village, when he was compelled to face up to the positions of the prophets, had prepared Rees Howells for the even greater light that came as his ministry reached out to the world.

The readings

The readings that follow are extracts from some of the college meetings and are mainly on Bible intercessors who were such an inspiration to Rees Howells as he reached out in faith in his worldwide ministry of intercession.

In dealing with the lives of the intercessors of the Bible Rees Howells invariably showed that a long period of preparation had usually taken place before the Almighty could bring them to the place where they were so much in his hands that they were complete instruments for the divine purpose of their intercession. Most of the readings have therefore been arranged in accordance with this pattern.

Moses

Stage 1: The Preparation
Moses was learned in all the wisdom of the Egyptians, and was mighty in deeds and in words.   Acts 7.22

Nothing in the life of Moses happened by chance. As an infant he was miraculously preserved from death and rescued by Pharaoh's daughter, and his own mother, who had risked her life to save him, became his nurse. God sent the princess down to the river that day and moved her to adopt the child as her own son. Moses had the best education that Egypt could give. He was probably the only person who could receive the Law from God and give it to the nation. See how the deliverer was being prepared.

Then came the day when he tried to deliver his own people himself and had to leave Egypt. He had made the great decision and identified himself with the people who were in bondage, and the writer of the letter to the Hebrews tells us, 'By faith, Moses, when he was come to years, refused to be called the son of Pharaoh's daughter; choosing rather to suffer affliction with the people of God, than to enjoy the pleasure of sin for a season; esteeming the reproach of Christ greater riches than the treasures of Egypt' (Hebrews 11.24–26). When God wanted to choose a deliverer, was there a better man than the one who had tried to do it of his own accord? God will not use you until he sees that you are prepared to act yourself, and he will always find the one who carries the biggest burden. Moses always knew why he was living in Midian for those 40 years – because he had tried to deliver God's people. God had made a covenant with Abraham, with Isaac and with Jacob. Was there another man in the nation he could have used to carry out that covenant?

In the early chapters of Exodus we read of 40 years of a man's life. The wonderful steadiness of Moses in the tests in Egypt, with Pharaoh, the magicians and his own people, was due to the 40 years of death-life in Midian. The prince in Egypt became the shepherd of his father-in-law's sheep in the desert. You cannot be steady in a test while there is flesh undealt with, but Moses knew that his life had been forfeited and anything God would give him after that was better than death.

Stage 2: The Call
I am the God of thy father, the God of Abraham, the God of Isaac, and the God of Jacob . . . I have surely seen the affliction of my people which are in Egypt . . . and I am come down to deliver them . . . Come now therefore and I will send thee unto Pharaoh that thou mayest bring forth my people, the children of Israel, out of Egypt.   Exodus 3.6–8, 10

One morning when Moses was about his ordinary business, he saw a burning bush and turned aside to see what it was. From the midst of the bush God spoke to him: 'I have surely seen the affliction of my people . . . and have heard their cry . . . for I know their sorrows. Come now therefore and I will send thee unto Pharaoh that thou mayest bring forth my people . . . out of Egypt.' And Moses said, "Who am I that I should go unto Pharaoh and that I should bring forth the children of Israel out of Egypt?"' (Exodus 3.6–11)

After those 40 years in Midian, Moses was not the man who had tried to deliver the people himself. God had so dealt with him during those years that all self-confidence had gone. God had to overcome his objections, one by one, until finally Moses accepted the commission. From that moment Moses changed from the realm of man to the realm of God. Everything changed: his ideas, his whole outlook, his very world. From then on he became responsible before God for this nation of two million people. So he turned his back on Midian and faced the task in Egypt.

Stage 3: The Deliverer (1)
And it came to pass by the way in the inn, that the Lord met him, and sought to kill him.   Exodus 4.24

Why did the Lord seek to kill Moses? Whatever happened in the inn, do you think that if God had worked on a man all his lifetime in order to use him, that he would allow that man to stand in his way? Once you have given up the treasures of Egypt that is not your test afterwards. While Moses was in Midian, he knew very well that if he had remained in Egypt he would have been killed, but once he came into God's plan, he was no longer his own. If this man would disobey or do wrong he would have set back God's plan for a thousand years. The devil knew that if he could get Moses he would get the nation. If a man is God's channel, he will watch him every second of the day, but that man must have given himself up to God completely. Undoubtedly Moses did that. Was it the test of the circumcision? At any rate Moses lost his wife and his sons here.

Stage 3: The Deliverer (2)
And Pharaoh said, 'Who is the Lord that I should obey his voice to let Israel go?   Exodus 5.2
But they hearkened not unto Moses for anguish of spirit and for cruel bondage.   Exodus 6.9

No one knew what it cost Moses in Egypt when the elders of Israel rejected him and Pharaoh drove him from his presence. God had said that he was coming down to deliver his people but that was known only to Moses. He could not convice the people or Pharaoh by word of mouth but he demonstrated to them the power of God. God had said he would make him a god to Pharaoh and from that time Moses acted as God. It was the faith of Moses that brought the plagues and it is as much as we can do to believe they happened. Finally God put Moses in a situation from which only he could deliver him. He was a man in an extremity and God always allows a man he has called to run to his extremity that he may know once and for all that he cannot do the thing himself. God had one more judgment to bring on Pharaoh, the death of the firstborn. Moses knew the very day they were to be delivered and he knew that the deliverance was to come by death. The Passover was the real beginning of Israel as a nation, after their years in

Egypt, but probably the people never understood the meaning of the blood on the doorposts.

Stage 3: The Deliverer (3)
Then sang Moses and the children of Israel this song unto the Lord, and spake, saying, 'I will sing unto the Lord for he hath triumphed gloriously: the horse and his rider hath he thrown into the sea.' **Exodus 15.1**

The nation had seen great wonders in Egypt but would they believe when it came to a personal test? After the victory at the Red Sea their song was a song of deliverance not a song of faith. They had failed completely in the test and they failed again at Marah where the bitter waters were made sweet. They failed in the wilderness where God gave them manna and again at Rephidim where they saw Moses walk up to the rock and water came forth. Moses took twelve men with him and he believed that the God who created nature could handle the laws of nature.

At Sinai the nation came into direct touch with God for the first time. Three months after leaving Egypt they were now alone in the wilderness with God. They had not really known what he was like and now he revealed himself as Almighty God and they heard him speak to Moses in an audible voice. They meant to do what he asked of them because he had delivered them from bondage, but fear came because they could not stand his holiness. What a wonderful offer he made to these people – to be a peculiar treasure to him – but his presence put a restraint, upon them. They all had the offer to be a sanctified people but they failed in every test in the wilderness.

Stage 4: The Intercessor (1)

And the Lord said unto Moses . . . 'Let me alone that my wrath may wax hot against them, and that I may consume them: and I will make of thee a great nation.' And Moses besought the Lord his God . . . and the Lord repented of the evil which he thought to do unto his people.   Exodus 32.9, 10, 11, 14

These people had been involved in all that had taken place since they left Egypt. God had given them the manna and water from the rock. Now they watched Moses going up Mount Sinai to meet the God whose presence and glory were manifest there – and in six weeks they were worshipping the golden calf. How great is the power of the devil over fallen human nature. Aaron, the second-in-command, was the man who fashioned the golden calf. The leadership had not cost him what it cost Moses. His weaknesses and failure did not become apparent until he was left alone. It is always possible to shield yourself under your leader. Moses went up the mountain and left Aaron in charge. Probably Aaron expected him back that night, but he did not come back. Unless the person who is dwelling in the leader is dwelling in you, when you are separated you would be like these people.

In one day, all that Moses had done in two years had come to nothing. When God said that he would destroy the nation, he meant it, and Moses knew it. Never before in a crisis, such as at the Red Sea, had Moses offered himself as a mediator, but now he stood between the wrath of God and the people. He had the offer to take the place of Abraham to be the founder of a new nation, but he refused. All personal ambition had gone long before. He was responsible for these people, and the man who has accepted a commission from God has authority with him. 'God repented of the evil which he thought to do unto his people.' Who made him repent? There is a position of authority with God and when you come there you prevail upon him.

But when Moses came down from the mountain and saw the sin which the people had committed, he went on to God's side against them. He told the Levites each to kill his brother, his friend, his son, and three thousand died. But even this did not clear the guilt of the sin. God is merciful and longsuffering, but he cannot clear the guilty without an atonement. Moses knew that God could cast them out of his presence for ever, and so he returned to Mount Sinai.

———◆———

And Moses returned unto the Lord and said, 'Oh, this people have sinned a great sin, and have made them gods of gold. Yet now, if thou wilt forgive, their sin – and if not, blot me I pray thee out of thy book which thou hast written.'   Exodus 32.31, 32

Moses said, 'Peradventure I shall make an atonement for your sin.' *Atonement*: there is no word in the Bible so sweet as that word. When you make an atonement you must pay the very penalty that the one who sinned would have to pay. Again Moses went up the mountain and he was on his face before God for another 40 days and nights. Again he pleaded the convenant that God had made with Abraham. Finally he said, 'Forgive their sin – and if not, blot me out of thy book.' We shall have to wait for eternity to know how far Moses meant this.

———◆———

And the Lord said unto Moses, 'Whosoever hath sinned against me, him will I blot out of my book. Therefore now go, lead the people unto the place of which I have spoken unto thee; behold, mine Angel shall go before thee . . . for I will not go up in the midst of them; for thou art a stiffnecked people: lest I consume thee in the way. Exodus 32.33, 34, 33.3

See how Moses prevailed again. God spoke to him face to face and said, 'My presence shall go with thee and I will give thee rest.' God the Creator met Moses on the Mount and came down to meet the deliverer of the nation. He prevailed on God to go with them and then went further still and asked to be allowed to see his glory. Then God made a covenant that he would drive out the inhabitants of the land before them. So when the nation faced entering the promised land, it was not the giants and the walled cities that turned them back – they disbelieved the covenant.

Stage 4: The Intercessor (2)
And the children of Israel saw the face of Moses, that the skin of Moses' face shone: and Moses put the veil upon his face again, until he went in to speak to him. Exodus 34.35

The second time Moses came down from the Mount not a single person could look on his face. He had been in the presence of God 40 days and nights. The tabernacle had been put outside the camp and from this time Moses spent all his time in the tabernacle. Without the intercession of Moses, God would not have gone with the people any further, but as the intercessor, Moses brought God again into their midst. He had been a leader before: now he was an intercessor. One man prevailed to bring a spiritual blessing to the people. When the tabernacle was to be built, in the end the people had to be restrained from bringing materials, they brought so much. Their whole attitude had changed. One man's intercession had brought a nation back to God.

Whenever Moses went in to the tabernacle, the cloud came down and God shut him in with himself. It was there that Moses wrote the first five books of the Bible. There, in God's presence, he wrote as the Lord revealed to him the story of Creation and the history of his people.

Stage 5: The Wilderness Years (1)

And Moses said, 'Wherefore hast thou afflicted thy servant? and wherefore have I not found favour in thy sight, that thou layest the burden of all this people upon me? . . . I am not able to bear all this people alone, because it is too heavy for me.'   Numbers 11.11, 14

This is one of the few times you find weakness in the great prophet. I wonder whether this was the first position where he backslid? The people, so often murmuring, were dissatisfied with manna, the food which God had given them, and Moses was so disturbed on this occasion that he got into the state to question God, 'Am I a father to this people?' He had believed greater things than this before so why should he go under in this test? But if you have any failure in your life never criticise Moses, unless you have believed as much as he believed and beyond him. At this point his burden for the nation was such that he would rather die than not go through.

When Aaron and Miriam murmured against him, God upheld Moses and said, 'With this man I have spoken face to face,' and with no other did he do this.

The Word also says that 'the man Moses was very meek, above all the men which were upon the face of the earth' (Numbers 12.3). The rarest thing on earth is meekness, but Moses had been in personal touch with God himself, and no flesh can stand in his presence. Only God can change your nature and put meekness in place of pride. It costs to come into this spirit of meekness.

Stage 5: The Wilderness Years (2)

And the Lord said unto Moses, 'How long will this people provoke me and how long will it be ere they believe me? . . . I will smite them with the pestilence, and disinherit them, and will make of thee a greater nation and mightier than they' . . . and Moses said, 'Pardon, I beseech thee, the iniquity of this people according unto the greatness of thy mercy' . . . and the Lord said, 'I have pardoned according to thy word.' Numbers 14.11, 12, 19, 20

At Kadesh-barnea God judged the people on their own report. They had turned against him many times before and had been forgiven many times, but there comes a moment where you cannot get forgiveness. The writer to the Hebrews tells us that Esau came there. The 'old man' thinks he can continue to sin and get forgiveness but once God acts you cannot be reinstated.

These people never believed God. He will always test believing on a point where there is no other source of deliverance. Faith is the greatest weapon God has put in the hands of the believer but it must be a believing in the spirit. A believing that is only mental assent or of the senses will never hold out. People will always believe when there are signs but what kind of believing is that? Signs do not change people.

At Kadesh-barnea the people sinned against the covenant God had made at Sinai, that he would drive out the nations in the land before them. Only Caleb and Joshua believed, and God said that everyone of those who had disbelieved would never enter the land. Plague carried thousands away but plague never touched Caleb and Joshua. Would you think that these people with their persistent unbelief should enter the land? Moses prevailed again so that God did not destroy them at that time but they were never to enter the land. In despair they tried to go against the enemy but God was not with them, they were defeated and had to turn back into the wilderness.

Then came the rebellion of Korah, Dathan and Abiram, and 250 princes stood with them against Moses, claiming that God was as much with them as with him. Again Moses stood in the gap but all those who rebelled were destroyed. It was a great crisis but Moses told Aaron, as high priest, to take a censor with fire from the altar, and incense, and to go amongst the people to make an atonement, 'and he stood between the living and the dead and the plague stayed.'

Stage 5: The Wilderness Years: Conclusion
And Moses lifted up his hand and with his rod he smote the rock twice: and the water came out abundantly . . . And the Lord spake unto Moses and Aaron, 'Because ye believed me not, to sanctify me in the eyes of the children of Israel, therefore ye shall not bring this congregation into the land which I have given them.'
Numbers 20.11, 12
And I besought the Lord at that time saying, 'O Lord God . . . I pray thee, let me go over and see the good land that is beyond Jordan . . . but the Lord was wroth

with me for your sakes . . . and said, 'Let it suffice thee; speak no more unto me of this matter.'
Deuteronomy 3.23–26

The moment you limit God you do it once too many times. This is what Moses did at Meribah, and God turned him down. Whatever you do is not counted if by unbelief or disobedience you hinder God. Moses failed and was not to go one step further. He failed in the place where God offered victory. Three times he tried to get God to reverse his judgment but God could not do it. Moses had been commissioned to take the nation right in to the promised land but here he failed to believe God and to sanctify him in front of the people, and because of this he was barred from the land. How sad, that Moses fell, as well as Aaron and Miriam. Nevertheless the covenant still stood, and a new generation entered the land under Joshua and Caleb.
During those years in the wilderness, Moses taught the new generation the laws of the kingdom, the laws they were to obey when they entered the promised land. In the book of Deuteronomy we see him preparing the people for the time when they would go in to the land of Canaan. In chapter 32 is the song of Moses, calling not only the people but the heavens and the earth to give heed to his words. The years in the wilderness were years of testing, to prove what was in the nation before they went into the land.

Daniel

Stage 1: The Preparation
But Daniel purposed in his heart that he would not defile himself.   Daniel 1.8

Why, when thousands were taken to Babylon at the time of the Captivity, did God pick out these four young men, Daniel and his three companions? They were men who lived for God and not for themselves. What a chance these Jewish captives had: to be educated in the king's palace, to have the best of food and everything else. But Daniel did not think in this way. He 'purposed in his heart that he would not defile himself with the portion of the king's meat, nor with the wine which he drank.' This was the beginning of the young man who was to tell what would happen at the end of the age. You first prove God where you are or you will never prove him anywhere else. Once you enter that spiritual realm where Daniel was for three years, you never want to come out of it. When you are living 'within the veil' nothing can disturb you. You cannot take one natural thought or motive there. There was nothing in this world for Daniel to live for. He was a eunuch and lived on the plainest of food. Nothing in the palace attracted these four young men, and at the end of three years God gave them 'knowledge and skill in all learning and wisdom: and Daniel had understanding in all visions and dreams.' God gave them the very things on which the king would test them at the end of the three years, and they were then given authority and merit. God had refined them and changed them so that they lived for him and his glory alone in a heathen court.

Stage 2: The Interpreter
Then was the secret revealed unto Daniel in a night vision.   Daniel 2.19

The telling of dreams was a science in Babylon but

Daniel surpassed all the magicians, the astrologers, the sorcerers and the Chaldeans. Did Daniel know beforehand that he could give the interpretation of the dream? When God gave him an understanding in visions and dreams did it include telling the dream as well, when the dream was forgotten? How did Daniel know it? Only the king knew that what Daniel said was right. I do not believe that the magicians and the others believed it. They were only praising their gods that their lives were saved. The interpretation was such that it was difficult for any man to believe it, but Daniel convinced Nebuchadnezzar. He said, 'There is a God in heaven that revealeth secrets' and he gave God's plan for the Gentile world until the end of the age. What a scene! This great king, the 'head of gold', falling down in the presence of God and worshipping Daniel. Nebuchadnezzar realised that God was in Daniel.

We hear no more of this until the king had another dream. God was going to give Daniel the opportunity for everyone in Babylon to know of this. Daniel had to die to the first experience but there was to be a resurrection. There will always be a resurrection on a death. 'The tree that thou sawest . . . it is thou, O King, . . . they shall drive thee from men and thy dwelling shall be with the beasts of the field . . . till thou know that the Most High ruleth in the kingdom of men and giveth it to whomsoever he will' (Daniel 4.20, 25). The magicians did not believe before but now they would talk over Daniel's words and wonder about them until they were fulfilled a year later. Nebuchadnezzar had been exalted by his success and how difficult it was to tell him of the judgment that was to befall him.

Again in chapter 5, Daniel was given yet another chance to interpret to Belshazzar the writing on the wall. How God revealed himself through this man and showed that it was he who was ruling in the affairs of men! Was it

Daniel's intercession that brought judgment on Belshazzar? He not only convinced Nebuchadnezzar and Belshazzar that God was speaking to them through him but he convinced Darius and Cyrus also.

The Fiery Furnace
Our God whom we serve is able to deliver us from the burning fiery furnace, and he will deliver us out of thine hand, O king. But if not, be it known unto thee, O king, that we will not serve thy gods nor worship the golden image which thou hast set up.   Daniel 3.17, 18

The ordinary people were not called to the dedication of the image that Nebuchadnezzar had set up. What a position these three young men were in. They believed the Word through Isaiah, 'When thou walkest through the fire thou shalt not be burned' (Isaiah 43.2), and they walked with God into an impossibility. They had a chance to be a blessing not only in Babylon but to millions of people after them. Even without deliverance they said they would not worship the golden image. Unless everything in you has died and you are on the altar, you will save your life 100 per cent. These men went into that furnace not to be burned but for victory. God will not deliver on the point of a challenge unless there is faith, and God will only use you on a point of proved faith. These three young men raised up a standard of faith – that it could 'quench the violence of fire' (Hebrews 11.34).

Stage 3: The Intercessor (1)
This Daniel was preferred above the presidents and

princes because an excellent spirit was in him; and the king thought to set him over the whole realm. Then the presidents and princes sought to find occasion against Daniel concerning the kingdom; but they could find none occasion nor fault; neither was there any error or fault found in him. Then said these men, 'We shall not find any occasion against this Daniel except we find it against him concerning the law of his God.'

Then the king commanded and they brought Daniel and cast him into the den of lions . . . Daniel was taken up out of the den and no manner of hurt was found upon him, because he believed in his God. Daniel 6.3, 4, 5, 16, 23

What did it mean to a man who had gone to a country as a captive to rise to such a position that God could rule Babylon through him? The great figures of all time have been the Jewish people. God will not use a shallow man. What a wonderful life this man lived that his enemies could find no fault in him. There is nothing like a life of depending upon God for daily needs to walk uprightly.

Daniel knew the law and even the king was not above the law of the Medes and Persians. There was no need for Daniel to challenge the law in the open. It was only for 30 days and he may have taken some time to decide to challenge it. The 'old man' is always strong until he is challenged and then he will try to trust God when there is no test, but fail when there is. You are what you are in a test. Daniel convinced a heathen king of the holiness and almightiness of God. In doing what he did, Daniel knew he was challenging the lion's den. The king was displeased with himself because he had been led astray and stood to lose the man in whom he had confidence. As a rule you do not know how far a challenge will go. Did it go further than Daniel expected? Could not deliverance come from the king? It could not. But the king said, 'Thy God whom thou servest continually, he will deliver you.' If the Spirit of God is in you, others will know it. Pharaoh recognised it in Joseph and here it was repeated in Daniel. What a night Daniel spent in the lions' den! 'My God hath sent his angel and hath shut the lions' mouths.' When God finds one person testing and proving a position of faith, that one stands out through eternity. Darius published his decree that thoughout his kingdom men should reverence the God of Daniel.

Stage 3: The Intercessor
I, Daniel, understood by books . . . whereof the word of the Lord came to Jeremiah the prophet, that he would accomplish seventy years in the desolations of Jerusalem. And I set my face unto the Lord God, to seek by prayer and supplications, with fasting and sackcloth and ashes.   Daniel 9.2, 3

In Babylon Daniel came up stage by stage until he could believe for the deliverance of the nation. When did God begin to prepare for this deliverance: at the end of the 70 years or at the beginning? Daniel was now an old man but he had lived a blameless life in the court of the kings of Babylon and now he was to be an intercessor for his people. During those years the great revelations of the future were given until the time came for him to pray the people back to their land in accordance with the prophecy of Jeremiah. His life was forfeit after the experience of the lions' den and he lived only for the glory of God and for his will.

These things are not brought about in any automatic way and Daniel had to 'set himself to seek God for the fulfilment of Jeremiah's prophecy' by prayer and fasting and supplications. There was nothing of self in that wonderful prayer. He identified himself with his people in their sin and apostacy and pleaded for forgiveness, that God's righteous anger might be abated, and he ended with the cry from his inmost being, 'O Lord, forgive; O Lord, hearken and do; defer not for thine own sake, O my God: for thy city and thy people are called by thy name.' Is it any wonder that the reply came with assurance that his prayer had indeed been heard? He lived on into the reign of Cyrus, King of Persia, and saw the beginning of the fulfillment of the prophecy.

'Now in the first year of Cyrus, king of Persia, that the word of the Lord spoken by the mouth of Jeremiah might be accomplished, the Lord stirred up the spirit of Cyrus, king of Persia, that he made a proclamation throughout all his kingdom . . . Thus saith Cyrus, king of Persia, "All the kingdoms of the earth hath the Lord God of heaven given me; and he hath charged me to build a house in Jerusalem which is in Judah. Who is there among you of all his people? The Lord his God be with him and let him go up." ' (2 Chronicles 36.22, 23.)

Queen Esther

Stage 1: The Preparation
Esther was brought also into the king's house . . . Esther had not showed her people nor her kindred. And the king loved Esther above all the women, and she obtained grace and favour in his sight . . . so that he set the royal crown upon her head, and made her queen instead of Vashti.   Esther 2.8, 10, 17

How great this king, Artaxerxes, was! His kingdom stretched from India to Ethiopia. How could God reach a monarch as great as this? Who would have thought, after Vashti was removed, that Esther would be chosen above all the other maidens in that vast country, that a Jewess would occupy this, the highest position that any girl in the kingdom could have? How wonderful it was that God had put her in that place just at the right time! God is always ahead of the devil and he knew that the enemy through Haman planned to destroy the Jewish people. Who but the queen could have acted over the head of the king's chief minister, and one who had the law on his side?

Stage 2: The Crisis

When Haman saw that Mordecai bowed not, nor did him reverence, then was Haman full of wrath. And he thought scorn to lay hands on Mordecai alone: for they had shown him the people of Mordecai: wherefore Haman sought to destroy all the Jews that were throughout the whole kingdom.   Esther 3.5, 6

If it had come to the mind of Mordecai that through not bowing down to Haman the lives of all his people would be at stake, I wonder if he would still have refused? This is not the only time that the devil has tried to destroy the Jewish people. He tried in Egypt at the time of the birth of Moses, when Pharaoh commanded that the Hebrew children should be thrown into the Nile. He tried to destroy the Saviour when Herod ordered the slaughter of the Jewish infants. He has tried again in our own century when Hitler attempted to destroy the Jews in the extermination camps.

The king gave them into Haman's hands and the order went forth that on a certain day all the Jews, in every province, were to be killed. Think of Mordecai crying through the streets of Shushan! The order could not be withdrawn: it was sealed with the king's seal, and the laws of the Medes and Persians could not be changed. Mordecai realised that Esther was the only person who could intervene with the king. So he charged her, through Hatach, that 'she should go in unto the king to make supplication unto him, and to make request before him for her people.' But what a test for Esther! She had not been called into the king's presence for thirty days, and to enter without being called was to face certain death. But the challenge of Mordecai to her was, 'Think not that thou shalt escape more than all the Jews. For if thou altogether holdest thy peace at this time then shall there enlargement and deliverance arise to the Jews from another place' (Esther 3.13, 14).

Stage 3: The Intercession
Who knoweth whether thou art come to the kingdom for such a time as this.
Fast ye for me, and neither eat nor drink three days, night or day: I also and my maidens will fast likewise: and so will I go in unto the king, which is not according to the law: and if I perish, I perish.   Esther 4.14, 16

Think what it cost these people to go through. Before God will use you in intercession it will cost you. If anyone had known a way of escape would they not have paid any price for deliverance? The fasting is not the point – it was the burden to be carried. When you face death neither food nor anything else will appeal to you. Fear turns away the need for food. We do not enter into the experience of these people because we are not in a similar position. Esther was not only facing death: she

121

would have to disclose the fact that she herself was a Jewess. Can you see that volume of prayer going up for those three days from the Jews while their queen was facing death? They knew that unless she prevailed they would all die. This is what I mean by a real death. This young woman was giving her life for the nation. Could the throne refuse that cry? These people raised up a standard to be a channel for God.

Stage 4: The Victory
And the king held out to Esther the golden sceptre that was in his hand. So Esther drew near and touched the top of the sceptre. Then said the king unto her, 'What wilt thou, Queen Esther, and what is thy request? It shall be even given thee to the half of my kingdom.'
Esther 5.2, 3

How near the enemy came in this situation! Even Esther could not go through the first time. She had to stand against the king's chief minister. She failed the first day, and so would anyone. This shows what it cost to do it, but she went through the second time and threw her all into it. Haman discerned nothing of what God had prepared for him. What a show God made of the devil in Haman and what a deliverance for the Jews! Even so the king nearly had a civil war on his hands, and hundreds who opposed the Jews were killed. How great was the victory!

When we enter into our king's presence shall we be able to prevail as Esther prevailed? You will never enter into that presence with a shade of anything between you and God. Your victories will be as real as your deaths. If the enemy has any hold over you, you will not prevail. Unless your death is as real as Queen Esther's, you will not prevail to deliver others.

Ezekiel
And thou shalt speak my words unto them, whether they will hear or whether they will forbear: for they are most rebellious.   Ezekiel 2.7
For I have laid upon thee the years of their iniquity . . . so shalt thou bear the iniquity of the house of Israel. Ezekiel 4.5

People have not understood the ways of God with these men. A carnal mind never sees anything in intercession, but what great things these men did for the nation of Israel. Unless God takes hold of a man he will not carry this sort of burden. Ezekiel became willing for God to use him to show the nation what was going to happen to them, and he became an object lesson to a people who otherwise would not listen to him. He was only to speak when God spoke through him, and he was made a watchman to the house of Israel. Only a man with a unique revelation of God, a man into whom the Spirit of God entered, could have done what Ezekiel did. He was to bear the iniquity of his people. God laid it upon him, and what a path he had to walk. Death was to touch him in his own home: his wife would be taken from him but he was not to mourn for her, even as would happen to the people in the final fall of Jerusalem. God said he was making Ezekiel a sign to his people, and what deaths he went through. How many would be willing to be made a sign for the sake of the kingdom of God! No wonder Ezekiel had the revelation of the re-gathering of Israel, the restoration of the kingdom and the judgment of the nations. How much deeper this is than just a full surrender. This is God himself speaking to his people through his chosen channel, a man completely in his hands.

Hosea
And I will betroth thee unto me for ever: yea I will betroth thee unto me in righteousness, and in judgment, and in loving kindness and in mercies.   Hosea 2.19
How shall I give thee up, Ephraim? How shall I deliver thee, Israel?   Hosea 11.8

There are times when you cannot fathom the depths of God's love, a love higher than the heavens, the love of God for a lost world. Israel was a harlot like the wife of Hosea. Did he really love her? Could he love her in the same way after she left him? That is what Israel did to God. The love of Hosea might break on that point: it was as shadow to substance compared with God's love. To some of the Rabbis, Hosea is the greatest of the prophets because of the revelation of the love of God through him.

Isaiah
And the Lord said, 'Like as my servant Isaiah hath walked naked and barefoot three years for a sign and wonder . . .'   Isaiah 20.3

It is only in the light God shows you that you can understand this. Would you allow yourself to be a sign if you had the choice? Would you walk as Isaiah walked? How great these men were! When the Lord had me to go through the Bible from cover to cover, anything he would call me to do, as the prophets had done, I was to do it. I was alway afraid of Isaiah, but it was to be a Nazirite that the Lord called me.

The Apostle Paul

I say the truth in Christ, I lie not, my conscience also bearing me witness in the Holy Ghost, that I have great heaviness and continual sorrow in my heart. For I could wish myself were accursed from Christ for my brethren, my kinsmen according to the flesh: Romans 9.1–3

This man had such a burden for his own people that he said he would be willing to be accursed for their sake, if that would save them. Only one man before him said a thing like that – Moses. God has not made this test too plain so that men will not dabble with it. The apostle fulfilled his own word and 'laid aside every weight to run this race and win this prize'. He said, 'What things were gain to me those I counted loss for Christ. Yea, doubtless, and I count all things but loss for the excellency of the knowledge of Christ Jesus, my Lord: for whom I have suffered the loss of all things and do count them but dung that I may win Christ' (Philippians 3.7, 8, 9), and again, 'That I may know him, and the power of his resurrection, and the fellowship of his sufferings, being made conformable unto his death' (Philippians 3.10).